Hugo L. Black

and the Dilemma of American Liberalism

Justice Hugo L. Black
1886–1971

Hugo L. Black

and the Dilemma of American Liberalism

Tony Freyer

Edited by Oscar Handlin

SCOTT, FORESMAN/LITTLE, BROWN HIGHER EDUCATION
A Division of Scott, Foresman and Company
Glenview, Illinois London, England

Acknowledgment

Frontispiece photo: used with permission of the University of Alabama School of Law

Library of Congress Cataloging-in-Publication Data

Freyer, Tony Allan.
Hugo L. Black and the dilemma of American liberalism / Tony Freyer.
p. cm.—(The Library of American biography)
ISBN 0-673-39951-6
1. Black, Hugo LaFayette, 1886–1971. 2. Judges—United States—Biography. I. Title. II. Series.
KF8745.B55F74 1990 347.73'2634—dc20
[B]
[347.30735343]
[B]

89-24358
CIP

Printed in the United States of America.

1 2 3 4 5 6 — EBL — 94 93 92 91 90 89

To Zu and Allan, again.

The men who create power make an indispensable contribution to the Nation's greatness, but the men who question power make a contribution just as indispensable, especially when that questioning is disinterested, for they determine whether we use power or power uses us.

John F. Kennedy
October 26, 1963, Amherst College

Editor's Preface

Hugo Black grew to manhood in a South pulled by contradictory forces. On one hand, the region still held on to the romantic vision of a gallant civilization, doomed by the Civil War. On the other hand, it also felt the impact of industrialization that created a new modern South. Pressures from both sides influenced the young man's thinking.

Black was born into a middle-class Alabama family. He set forth early in life, pursuing the field of law to make a career between business and government. Gregarious and sociable by nature, he drifted into politics and thoughtlessly accepted membership in the Ku Klux Klan.

When Black arrived in Washington as a senator from Alabama, his ideas, though tinged with populism, still had not taken clear form. The Depression and the New Deal, though, transformed his attitudes. The long economic crisis demanded positive state action, and elements in the population, until then unheard, voiced grievances that could not be disregarded. The pressure of modern issues forced Black to feel his way toward a more comprehensive vision of justice.

Like many of the other turns in his life, Black's appointment to the Supreme Court was more a matter of happenstance than of grand design. Franklin Delano Roosevelt could not have predicted that Black, who was neither a legal scholar nor a profound thinker, would play such an important role in slowly working out a vision of the way the Court could help transform American society. In working hard and applying common sense to unprecedented problems, however, Black helped redefine the constitutional meanings of liberty and equality. The painful steps taken in that direction form the framework of Professor Freyer's thoughtful book.

Oscar Handlin

Acknowledgments

I am grateful to Oscar Handlin for suggesting this contribution to the Library of American Biography. Dean Charles Gamble and his successor, Dean Nathaniel Hansford, of the University of Alabama School of Law provided indispensable financial support. Law Library Director Cherry Lynn Thomas and acquisitions librarian Paul Pruitt, gave essential assistance in many ways. Also, without the careful assistance of the School of Law's clerical staff, the writing would have been considerably more difficult. I continue to be thankful for the access provided by Professor Paul Freund to the Louis Brandeis and Felix Frankfurter Papers located at Harvard Law School's Manuscript Division; and to Dr. David Wigdor, who opened my way to the Justice Hugo Black Papers in the manuscripts division of the Library of Congress. Justice Black's first law clerk, Jerome A. Cooper, always gave generously of his time whenever I asked. It is also a privilege to have talked with Mrs. Elizabeth Black, Hugo Black, Jr., and Mrs. Mildred Black Faucett.

From 1983 to 1986, I directed the University of Alabama School of Law's commemoration of Justice Black's birth. During 1987 and 1988 I prepared for publication the proceedings of two conferences that were part of this commemoration, and also wrote this book. Long before these responsibilities and opportunities came my way, however, Black had made an impression on me. In the mid-1960s I recall clearly my high school government teacher reading a handwritten letter Black sent in reply to a letter from a member of the class. Almost immediately I forgot the details, but throughout the succeeding years the substance of Black's comments remained vivid: he had an abiding respect for America's past, a pervading trust in the nation's future, and a profound grasp of the strengths and weaknesses of human character connecting the past, present, and future, sustaining reason for hope. No doubt this had some influence on me as I studied and wrote about Black's life.

I am fortunate to have such fine friends and colleagues as Kenneth C. Randall and Howard Jones, whose reading of portions of the manuscript saved me from errors. I am also grateful to Francis N. Stites; yet again he responded to my call for help by reading the whole manuscript through with interest and considerable attention. The greatest debt is to Forrest and Ellen McDonald, whose thorough comments and criticisms have made this a better book and, hopefully, its author a better writer. The interest of my colleagues at the University of Alabama School of Law, and the work of the contributors to the Justice Black Centennial, which I have drawn upon extensively, are much appreciated. Of course, only I am responsible for what is finally here written.

The dedication is to my wife, a teacher herself, and to my son, with love.

Tony Freyer

Contents

Hugo L. Black

and the Dilemma of American Liberalism

CHAPTER ONE

Clay County Populism (1886–1907)

Hugo Black often returned in his thoughts to Ashland, Clay County, Alabama, a small, isolated town in the Appalachian foothills near the Georgia border, where he grew up amid memories of the Civil War and Reconstruction—and of the conquering national government. Everyone depended on the land on which they raised corn and cotton, either as farmers or sharecroppers. A few residents, like Black's father, were merchants providing goods and credit. The county was remote enough so that no railroad connected it directly with Birmingham, the state's new, growing industrial center, and only politics brought events of the outside world. Although government usually seemed far away, a struggle between Alabama's northern and southern sections touched everyone; indeed, entwined in this conflict were citizens' hopes and fears about economic opportunity, religion, and relations between whites and blacks.

These rural roots influenced Black's involvement in twentieth-century American liberalism. The liberal tradition that emerged out of the Populist Revolt and Progressive movement during his formative years incorporated diverse strands. Distrust of special privilege and concentrated wealth and power, and a paternalistic government sympathetic and responsive to the plight of the common man, were central to liberalism. But it embodied a profound dilemma. Many liberals rejected the traditional fear of big government in favor of a new reliance on scientific management and bureaucracy. Others including Black remained distrustful of increased government authority, convinced that continuing confrontation between the few and the many, the rich and the poor, demonstrated that no one could be trusted with power, not even if administered in a scientific, disinterested manner. Throughout his public career, Black wrestled with the dilemma: whether the benefits of big government justified its drawbacks. The values learned in Clay County shaped both his defeats and his triumphs.

Born in Harlan, a hamlet of Clay County, on February 27, 1886 to locally prominent and respected parents, Hugo, named by his mother after the French writer Victor Hugo, was nearly four when his family moved ten miles to Ashland, the county seat. Fayette Black, his father, had joined the Confederate Army at fourteen, then returned home to Clay County after the Civil War to become a storekeeper like his own father. The population of Ashland during Hugo's childhood and youth was about 350. There he lived until 1903, when he left to continue his education, first in Birmingham and then in Tuscaloosa at the University of Alabama School of Law. In 1906 he returned to Ashland to begin a law practice, but found so little business that at the end of 1907 he returned to Birmingham.

During the mid-1870s and mid-1890s severe depressions rocked the nation, while cities such as Birmingham grew faster than country places like Clay County. The proportion of rural Americans dropped from 72 percent in 1880 to less than 65 percent in 1890. Through his father's mercantile business, young Black and his family felt these pressures arising from the depressions and social dislocation. In early spring Fayette Black extended farmers credit for provisions, equipment, supplies, and seeds. The price of cotton was 20¢ a pound in 1870; in 1880 it had fallen to 10¢ and during the 1890s it went down to 6¢. In that period an acre of cotton paid no more than $18 and corn brought only $10.91, while the cost of fertilizer alone was $40 a ton. Modest Clay County farms, worked by the families owning them and by tenants or sharecroppers, rarely made a profit except during boom years.

Because credit bound together the merchant, his family, and the farming community, everyone suffered during bad times, though not equally. All were vulnerable to railroad rates, weevils, drought, the interest charged by northern big-city financiers, and above all the fluctuating prices of international staple markets. Indeed, the local merchant depended on big urban wholesalers for the credit he provided his neighbors. Yet the merchant could protect himself by charging rates of interest as high as 50 to 75 percent and by acquiring a mortgage on the farmer's land or a lien on his crop. Many, including Fayette, commonly carried the farmer for as long as possible. In the long run foreclosures or excessive enforcement of liens undermined the agricultural system on which everyone depended. At the same time extensive ties of kinship and friendship linked the merchant and his debtors, creating another disincentive to arbitrary legal action.

The merchant's willingness to carry his neighbors and kinsmen through hard times enhanced his community standing and wealth. Over the long term his economic position benefited as he gradually acquired title to his debtors' lands. When Fayette Black died in 1899 he was among the county's largest property holders. Although the estate was divided among seven members of the senior Black's immediate family, Hugo's portion was large enough to pay for most of law school, finance the attempt at practicing in Ashland, and cover his move to Birmingham in 1907. It made sense for those in Fayette Black's position to play the role of community benefactor, helping rather than hounding the unfortunate. By sharing his customers' burdens merchant Black earned, if not affection, at least respect, which in a small town counted for much. That his risk was not as great as his customers' was less apparent than the fact that his own family's and the community's welfare were nonetheless interdependent.

The interplay between credit and social relations encompassed politics. Black's business partner was one of the most powerful Democratic party bosses in Clay County, leader of the conservative Democrats, including the state's powerful business group, known as Big Mules because of their "pull." The bosses influenced local affairs everywhere in Alabama. Many country merchants such as Black's partner used their economic clout to political advantage and often extended their customers' credit in order to win votes. Usually the exchange of credit for votes resulted from the subtle ties of social relations, but during the 1890s the political and social pressures became more overt.

Alabama's Populist movement coincided with Hugo's formative years. Alabama Populists drew support primarily from farmers who had lost or were about to lose their status as independent landowners. The slide to tenancy and its consequent dependency eroded economic welfare and self-respect. To meet the threat, Populists attempted to join forces with black tenants and farmers. The Populists also distrusted public authority and yet sought stronger government to remedy economic ills and to check corporate power and privilege. However, economic vulnerability undermined support for the higher property taxes which would have been required to pay for increased regulation. The paradoxical advocacy of limited and enlarged government posed a dilemma the Populists never resolved. Since the Populists included the very people whose property merchant Black gradually acquired, Hugo's father firmly opposed the third-party movement.

The bosses countered with appeals to the Jeffersonian distrust of big government, attachment to states' rights, and the memory of Republican-led federal intervention during Reconstruction. Fundamentally, however, the conservative Democrats proclaimed themselves the party of white supremacy. Emphasizing that Populist candidates advocated equal civil rights for whites and blacks, the bosses cried: "Who can look upon the fair and lovely women of this land and endorse this principle and the man who maintains it?" This political struggle increased racial tensions; during 1891 and 1892 alone forty-eight blacks in Alabama were lynched.

The Populist influence gradually declined after William Jennings Bryan's inglorious defeat in 1896. Yet the Populist Revolt shaped race relations during Hugo Black's early years. In Clay County by 1890 there were 14,601 whites and 1,704 blacks, but in the state's fertile black-belt counties blacks constituted a substantial majority of the population, and they retained political power through the right to vote until 1901. Throughout these years political leaders and their constituents in north Alabama, although they assumed that racial separation was appropriate on the basis of social custom, nonetheless supported civil rights for blacks as a matter of law. Black-belt whites, however, pushed a campaign to establish legally enforced racial segregation. As support for the Populists spread throughout places such as Clay County, the conservative Democrats throughout the state, including the black belt, called for segregation imposed by law. In 1901 the conservatives triumphed when Alabamians ratified a constitution incorporating racial segregation as a fundamental principle. This victory destroyed equal rights before the law, reducing blacks to second-class citizenship.

Young Hugo Black's experience with these conflicts was significant, albeit complex. Around the kitchen table, the center of family life, he heard politics discussed regularly. As a child and adolescent Hugo knew that his father described himself as a "Grover Cleveland Democrat" and, therefore, a conservative. Even as a toddler Hugo espoused his father's party preference, growing angry if someone observed, "You are a Populist, a third party-ite." Party identification and rivalry were important to the lives of most Americans during the late nineteenth century, and especially to locally prominent people like the Blacks. Thus as Hugo grew up working in the store or traveling about Clay County visiting friends and kinfolk, he was identified not only as the son of an important merchant but also in terms of his father's party affiliation.

Yet he recalled vividly his parents' rejection of the bosses' racial demagoguery. During one summer of Black's boyhood a racial tragedy rocked Ashland. A young black, who at times had taken Hugo for wheelbarrow rides, joined white boys in a creek, swimming. One of the whites demanded that the black leave the water, whereupon the boy responded angrily. Because he had been "sassed" the white ran home for his gun, and when he returned he shot the black dead. Because the murderer was the son of a prominent family the local judge took no action even though virtually the entire community acknowledged the white youth's guilt. The tragedy so angered Fayette Black that in the next election, for the first and only time, he voted for a Populist against the offending judge. On another occasion an elderly Negro working in the Black family's store delivered a parcel at the back door. Martha Black told her youngest son to bring the old man into the kitchen for some food. This sort of hospitality between the races was customary among genteel whites but contrary to entrenched social custom among the lower classes to whom the bosses appealed against the Populists. Black remembered these incidents for the rest of his life.

In addition, factional conflicts among the Democrats encouraged resistance in Clay County. The 1901 constitution empowered local officials to determine voter qualifications by literacy tests, poll taxes, and good character. When asked whether Christ and His disciples could register under such restrictions, a politician answered candidly: "That would depend entirely upon which way he was going to vote." The new constitution not only deprived blacks of the franchise but also reduced poor white voters by nearly 25 percent, particularly in Clay County.

The all-white primary further hurt the political influence of Black's home. Candidates chosen out of group struggles within the Democratic party left the victor in the primary virtually always winning the general election. Although blacks could no longer vote after passage of the 1901 constitution, they nonetheless counted as population in determining the number of each district's elected officials, giving the black belt proportionately more representatives than the north in statewide primary elections. The discriminatory political and constitutional measures reduced the political clout of Alabama's entire northern section, including Clay County.

From the Populists Hugo learned how to challenge the conservative bosses' primacy within the Democratic party. As a child and youth he attended every stump speech, parade, and rally, night or day, fair weather or foul. He stayed close to the polls until the last man voted and saw that effective oratory and direct personal appeals could inspire people to question the status quo. The Populists used these skills in many local elections. If in the long run their electoral triumphs were transitory, they nonetheless impressed upon young Black a basic, almost instinctive preference for the underdog. Once the white primary created essentially a one-party system in Alabama, any attempt to achieve political goals through rival party organizations became futile. The Populists taught Black the value of a constituency-oriented, face-to-face political style—however, their defeat revealed that in the future only Democratic candidates were likely to get elected by using it.

Black-belt bosses triumphed over north Alabama in the 1901 constitutional convention because they effectively manipulated popular faith in white supremacy. Once Jim Crow segregation triumphed, the more intense racial beliefs of the black belt acquired a primacy which public figures in north Alabama or elsewhere could little afford to challenge.

Religion also influenced Black's formative years. As far as young Hugo knew there were no Catholics or Jews in Clay County. Every church was of some Protestant denomination—including Methodist, Episcopalian, and Congregationalist, with the evangelical Baptist Church by far the largest. Although fragmented into numerous sects, Baptist congregations reflected and shaped the community's hopes and fears. Martha, Black's mother, insisted that her sons and daughters attend services every Wednesday night and Sunday. Central to these meetings were public confessions of sin and "speaking in tongues," an experience of spiritual ecstasy in which the speaker believed himself or herself a channel for the Holy Spirit. As long as he could remember, Black felt such public testimonials regarding individual weakness, given among a significant segment of the town's population, harmed reputations, caused personal pain, and reduced self-respect. Probably the most significant factor influencing Black's beliefs, however, was that his own father and two beloved uncles were publicly expelled from a Baptist congregation because they drank alcoholic beverages.

The church's influence extended beyond private affairs. It was often a significant factor in elections when ministers encouraged their congregations to vote for particular candidates and politicians used biblical language and stories to arouse the people's concern. Many evangelical protestant sects urged state and local governments to prohibit the manufacture and sale of alcoholic beverages, injecting government into the community's private life.

Prohibition acquired special meaning for Black at age sixteen, when his brother died. Pelham Black was one of Hugo's four brothers—athletic, handsome, popular with the ladies, and smart, having passed the Alabama state bar exam with the highest mark on record. One night while the twenty-two year old returned in the family horse and buggy after a social call, he fell asleep, whereupon the buggy overturned in a mill pond and Pelham drowned. The autopsy revealed that he probably was drunk.

The issue of alcohol touched young Hugo Black in other ways as well. Undoubtedly, his father's expulsion from the Baptist church created tensions for the family. Small, rural places like Ashland cherished respectability, believing that it was vital to social stability and responsible individual behavior. They were committed to personal independence and moral accountability. Ideally, the unity of the community and the rights of the individual reinforced one another. Respectability was integral to this balance because it liberated individuals from material or social dependency. Such independence was profoundly significant in a society intimately familiar with slavery and racial segregation.

As a successful merchant, Fayette Black was clearly entitled to respect as a pillar of ordered community life. In a society shaped by evangelical protestant proscriptions against the consumption of alcohol, however, his material success did not erase the consequences of what many regarded as a significant moral weakness. Thus merchant Black's antisocial indulgence threatened the community's vital moral order. The stigmatization of his father's reputation and Pelham's death strengthened Hugo's conviction that adherence to evangelical Christianity's moral code was necessary to the respectable individual conduct upon which the well-being of family and the community depended.

Black's mother reinforced this commitment to respectability. Her husband's drinking troubled Martha Black considerably, and Pelham's death intensified her concern. Although she was not herself a fundamentalist, she probably took the children to the Baptist church to maintain the family's reputation and also to instill the community's code of acceptable behavior. In addition, she urged young Hugo to follow in the footsteps of his older brother, Orlando, described at twenty-nine by *Notable Men of Alabama* as a "young physician of merit and promise." Martha noted with pride her son's increased social status after marrying an Episcopalian, even though Orlando himself remained a devoted Baptist throughout his life. She also heightened an awareness of respectability by seeing to it that her youngest son was the "neatest boy in Clay County."

The drive to maintain respectability probably also influenced Black's significant educational achievements. At four he learned to play the family organ well enough to perform at the local school's commencement, and the applause he received instilled a keen sensitivity to public attention. As he grew up, Black excelled in virtually every field of study the Clay county schools offered. Before the age of eighteen he demonstrated intellectual prowess at Birmingham's medical school by successfully completing a two-year program in one year. And since virtually every Ashland resident knew of the impressive academic and professional accomplishments of Black's two brothers, one a lawyer, the other a doctor, he was inspired to achieve public respect and recognition himself. Implicit in this individual ambition was also a determination to strengthen and preserve his family's place in the community.

The public education Black received in Ashland stressed the classics, Greek and Roman history and literature, and the cultural and political heritage of the Anglo-Saxon peoples. Strict discipline, too, was basic. Wherever appropriate the content of classwork and teaching emphasized moralistic and patriotic themes. Above all, the schools and the family relied on the Bible. Young Black and his peers often gave parable-like school presentations that either espoused fervent patriotism or defended religious and moral values against the temptations of alcohol and lawlessness. One speech aroused the mystical emotions associated with the Civil War and its aftermath:

> "There *was* a South of slavery and secession;
> That South, thank God, is dead;
> There is a South of Freedom and Union,
> That South, thank God, is living, breathing,
> growing every hour."

As Hugo won praise from family, peers, and the community for academic accomplishment, he undoubtedly absorbed the values of moral order, obedience to law, sobriety, discipline, social stability, and patriotism, all of which comprised the core of his education. But because he often preferred the company of books to that of people, Black acquired a reputation as a loner. While still quite young, perhaps before age ten, he began reading Charles Dickens, Walter Scott, and such literary classics as *Pilgrim's Progress.* Admittedly, he also consumed popular fiction and encountered what he later described as "sexually suggestive" and "openly obscene" material. Early on he acquired a firm independence of mind. He claimed that "an early familiarity with the obscene, dirty, profane, and pornographic language, instead of making me like it, had precisely the opposite effect. I have never liked either to use or read or hear language falling within these vague classifications." He accepted, to a point, then, the values inculcated by his family and education, but he determined for himself what priority to give them in his own life.

His youth instilled an ambivalent regard for individualism. The entwining of credit and social relations learned from his father's business taught young Black the extent to which individual and community life were interdependent. Domestic and international market pressures, the power struggle between north Alabama and the black belt, and the influence of urban financiers and railroads also fostered fears of dependency. Populist rhetoric emphasizing unity among independent agricultural producers—despite racial classification—heightened the belief that privileged classes, impersonal economic forces, and political exploitation threatened individual and thereby community welfare.

Anxieties arising from the ambiguous social standing of his family intensified Black's sensitivity to the individual's status *within* the community. Although he accepted the small-town code of moral and religious respectability, he rejected it as a basis for condemning his father, brother, and uncles. Nor could he condone the code when it potentially tarnished the personal reputations of innocent members of his family, including himself. One way to meet this challenge to respectability was to win community respect through academic achievement. This success also gave Black an inner strength to determine for himself how and to what extent he would apply community values to his own life.

The tension between individual and community values influenced Black's determination to become a lawyer. His interest in lawsuits was as constant and deeply rooted as his fascination with politics. The trials he attended made an impression lasting a lifetime. There he learned to appreciate the role of the jury in expressing community sentiments. Black learned probably the most profound lesson about law and community from the stand taken by a dear uncle whose son was murdered in cold blood. A posse formed to hang the murderer without a trial; but through a veil of tears the uncle told his neighbors to let the law take its course.

These experiences molded Black's goal. Only briefly did he question his decision to practice law after Pelham drowned and his mother urged him to become a doctor like his brother, Orlando. He attended medical school in Birmingham for a year, but told Orlando he believed he could better serve the community as a lawyer and a legislator representing Clay County in the Alabama legislature.

In 1904 at age eighteen, Black walked to a nearby town and took the train to Tuscaloosa where he entered the School of Law immediately. The institution was then small, having only two teachers. Instruction relied primarily upon lectures and questions and emphasized the common law, a body of rules, principles, and procedure inherited from England and adapted to the particular needs of each state in America. The core of the common law was a process of pleading that determined how issues were presented in court and resolved by the jury. Black knew that the jury was the repository of community values. In law school, he learned the tremendous influence lawyers exercised in determining whether an issue could get before the jury. An experienced lawyer could use pleading to protect his client, especially against an inexperienced opponent. In addition to the lectures, Black and his classmates learned the elements of the common law in moot courts. True to his preference for the underdog, he usually took the plaintiff's side in cases involving personal injury.

Besides the common law, the school's second principal focus of study was legislation. In 1887 Congress created the Interstate Commerce Commission to regulate the railroads, and in 1890 passed the Sherman Antitrust Act to protect farmers and small businessmen from large corporations. During the 1890s the Populists failed in their efforts to win stronger antitrust laws, more favorable credit policies, and stricter railroad regulation, but after the turn of the century the Progressives began enacting such measures at the state and federal level. As lawmakers intervened directly in social and economic affairs by imposing the system of racial segregation, they also considered statewide prohibition of the manufacture and distribution of alcohol. The principal legal basis for increased government intervention was the police power, a principle that traditionally sanctioned state responsibility for preserving community health, morals, and welfare.

Black graduated in 1906 near the top of his class with grades qualifying him for membership in Phi Beta Kappa. The University yearbook predicted he might one day sit upon the United States Supreme Court. In addition to these academic accomplishments, he kept alive an interest in politics as his classmates each year elected him secretary. The student yearbook described him as "one of those gentle souls that will use the devil himself with courtesy"; at another point it observed this "fellow seems to possess but one idea and that is a wrong one."

After graduation he returned to Ashland. Although the townspeople accepted Black with pride, they took their legal business to older lawyers. Generally he earned a small living investigating claims for insurance companies. Waiting for business that never came, Black continued to read widely in history, literature, and the classics, hoping to acquire a clearer understanding of human nature. Often he roamed the woods alone, practicing political and courtroom oratory. Seeking to gain clients and political contacts, Black joined the local Masonic lodge and the Knights of Pythias. He also became a member of the Ashland Baptist church, but only after the minister agreed that a public confession of religious faith or past sins was unnecessary. Black served the church as clerk, Sunday school teacher, and organist. He remained receptive to the basic moral code of evangelical protestantism, and no doubt hoped that membership might enhance his law practice and political prospects.

Before long, however, Black realized that the achievement of either his legal or his political ambitions was unlikely in Clay County. On a raw February day in 1907 a fire destroyed his modest office, and by September, the twenty-one year old had decided to leave home. With the remainder of his father's inheritance in his pocket, Hugo Black took the train again, this time seventy-five miles westward to Birmingham.

CHAPTER TWO

Progressivism in Birmingham (1907–1919)

❖
❖

In 1907, Birmingham was still a boom town. Just six years after Appomattox its founders had begun building upon the rich coal, iron, and limestone deposits a steel-producing city destined to rival its namesake in the English Midlands. In less than forty years Birmingham's mills and mines attracted nearly 133,000 residents, creating Alabama's largest urban center, but the rise to industrial prominence had a darker side. Nicknames such as "Bad Birmingham" and the "Murder Capital of the World" characterized a community troubled by persistent crime, periodic labor unrest, repeated racial and ethnic conflicts, and industrial accidents. Tensions aroused fears in the city's respectable citizens who supported Progressivism's increased governmental intrusion in the private lives of Birmingham's citizens.

In this environment Black thrived. Starting with few friends and no clients, within a decade he established one of the city's most successful law practices. During the same period he began to rise in Birmingham's progressive politics: appointed local criminal court judge at age twenty-five and three years later elected prosecutor of Jefferson County. This prominence was the outcome of considerable personal skill and determination and of the ability to conciliate the tension between individual accountability and community unity. It revealed, too, how far he was willing to subordinate individual liberty to community control.

In the beginning, he faced a future filled with risk and uncertainty. Following the pattern set in Ashland, he continued his self-education in the classics and history, reading such works as Gibbon's *Decline and Fall of the Roman Empire,* which reinforced a growing conviction that human nature was unchanging, though it would manifest itself differently in varying circumstances. Personally, his temperament continued to reflect the combination of a sincere, courteous sweetness with fixed convictions. He also displayed incorruptibility and singleness of purpose. His personal habits revealed evidence of his intensity: he smoked five packs of cigarettes a day but also excelled in tennis.

Above all, he started meeting people the day he got to Birmingham and never quit. New or continued memberships in the Masons, Knights of Pythias, and Odd Fellows were vital. As he had in Ashland he joined one of the city's largest places of worship, the First Baptist Church, where he taught hundreds of men in Sunday school. The determination to meet people also increased Black's friendships. Early on he met Herman M. Beck, a Jew and one of the city's foremost wholesalers. Beck, a high officer in the Knights of Pythias, asked Black to serve as his secretary during the year he held a statewide honorary office. "During the year I worked with him," Black wrote, "we became almost as close as father and son" and "I never knew a better or more honest man." In addition Black's early law partners extended his circle of contacts.

In the quest for business, Black learned the social landscape of Birmingham and Jefferson County. The majority of whites were of either English or Scotch-Irish descent, whereas blacks accounted for about 40 percent of the city's population. The next largest white ethnic group was German American, and there were also a fair number of Jews and Italians and a few Chinese and Syrians. Corresponding to ethnic differences were pronounced religious cleavages, particularly evangelical protestants versus Jews and Catholics.

Wealth and social standing further divided residents. In 1910 owners and managers of financial and industrial corporations constituted the top one percent of the population, with annual incomes ranging from $50,000 to more than a million dollars. The middle rank, including real estate, contracting, manufacturing, mercantile, and professional interests, comprised 19 percent of the population and had incomes of from $3000 to $35,000. Truck and dairy farmers, saloon and liquor dealers, retail grocers, artisans, various wage earners such as skilled craftsmen, clerical workers, coal miners, and unskilled workers and servants made up to 80 percent of the population, earning incomes of $500 or less. A young lawyer without social connections, Black belonged to the respectable middle rank, who nonetheless occupied a place above most community members.

Although the social elite commanded considerable informal influence and controlled exclusive institutions such as the Country Club, neither it nor its organizations operated as a cohesive political interest. Ethnic and religious groups from the middle and lower social strata, however, were politically mobilized. Evangelical protestant activists organized such associations as the Anti-Saloon League and the Law and Order League, lobbying for stricter regulation of Sunday observance, vice, and liquor. Middle- and lower-income white protestants also provided membership for reform movements such as the Alabama Anti-Convict Lease Association, and they made up the rank and file of the Ku Klux Klan. Minorities from the middle and lower social levels had their own political associations, such as the German-American Union and the Irish Democratic Club. Although Jews rarely formed lobbying organizations, they often supported other ethnic minorities against evangelical protestant activists. Other significant political divisions included a split between downtown and the suburbs and between rural Jefferson County and its urban core, Birmingham.

After 1901 blacks, generally poor and politically powerless, sank to second-class citizenship. Some whites from the upper and middle social groups, feeling little threat from blacks concerning jobs, supported limited equality before the law. Birmingham was, after all, located in north Alabama, where many whites continued to prefer racial separation based on social custom rather than on legal mandate. Blacks, approximately 40 percent of the free industrial work force, were vital to the community's prosperity. The system, whereby local law enforcement officials received no salaries but fees based on the number of legal notices served, litigations participated in, and arrests made, encouraged abuse, particularly the harassment of employed blacks. Consequently, a Chamber of Commerce official complained, "Negro laborers are continually being annoyed by officers of the law invading mines and furnace camps, night after night, looking for crap shooters, and those who are not arrested are demoralized through fear; consequently they work very irregularly. This evil can be modified only by the abolition of the fee system." At the same time, however, the Chamber of Commerce urged strict enforcement of vagrancy laws so that "Negroes are [not] allowed to loaf."

Hugo Black's rising law career conformed to these social realities. He welcomed and effectively represented clients from all ethnic, racial, religious, and economic groups, though most clients came from the middle and lower social strata. Moreover, although he was sympathetic to and freely defended individual Catholics, he distrusted the Church's power as an institution. Sunday school teaching put him in contact with hundreds of evangelical protestants, while some of the lodges he joined were nondenominational, electing as leaders Jews such as Beck. In addition, the great majority of white and black low-income workers composed a group of potential clients that an ambitious young lawyer could ill afford to ignore. Also, affiliation with middle- and low-income groups involved him in the vital center of local politics.

If extensive personal contacts were, Black wrote years later, "largely responsible for most of the cases I got in the first instance" there were "few cases I ever tried that did not bring me new business." Although he often represented injured plaintiffs or criminal defendants, Black resisted identification with a single set of clients. "During the time I was practicing in Birmingham," he wrote, "lawyers who represented labor unions made much more money out of representing individual members of the union than they did out of representing the unions themselves." Success in court gave such lawyers "prestige" in the community, which brought in the "business of non-union members and even business enterprises."

He learned early that a "practice that is too highly specialized sometimes causes a lawyer to adopt highly specialized or narrow views." This was "readily understandable with reference to 'corporation lawyers,'" he observed, "but it is wise to remember that 'labor lawyers' can be similarly molded." After receiving explicit authority to settle any disputes involving the company, Black represented "for some years on a very satisfactory basis" the Zurich Insurance Co. of Switzerland, "which did a large amount of business in the Birmingham vicinity." Moreover, although he represented United Mine Workers as a special attorney in quite a number of cases, he was never the union's regularly retained lawyer. He was, however, the regularly retained lawyer of the Carpenters' Union Local for many years, and also represented the Brotherhood of Railroad Trainmen in all of its business.

The diverse market for legal services shaped Black's preference for a general practice. During a violent strike in 1908 corporations supported by state authorities broke the unions, particularly the United Mine Workers. Little wonder that Black made much more money representing individual members than the unions. Craft unions composed of skilled workers such as trainmen and carpenters belonged to Birmingham's trade council, were racially segregated, and were part of the city's political structure. As the "regularly retained lawyer" for these unions, Black earned a steady income without threatening the status quo.

The case of *American Surety Company* v. *W. F. Pryor* suggested the diversity of clients. The Standard Oil Company employed Pryor as its Montgomery manager. When his department began reporting shortages the company claimed evidence of stealing and brought criminal charges against him. The American Surety Company was bound to pay the shortfall if Pryor did not. The case led to two jury trials in which Pryor received first $25,000 and then $50,000 in damages for harm to his reputation. The two corporations, however, pushed appeals until the Alabama Supreme Court decided against him. Even then, however, Black filed a sophisticated application for a rehearing and won his client a $50,000 judgment, thus demonstrating his legal ability.

Black's diverse clientele rarely included corporations. In urban areas with enough business to support specialization, a rough but pronounced split in the bar divided lawyers like Black, whose success depended on effective trial work representing individual plaintiffs before juries, from corporations that retained law firms on a more or less permanent basis. Unlike the plaintiff's lawyers, who served many different clients one case at a time, corporate attorneys became expert in areas of law relating to large, incorporated enterprise. A common litigation involved personal injury in which a maimed plaintiff sued the corporation for damages, arguing that the harm occurred because of the company's negligence. The jury decided whether the facts warranted recovery and, if so, what amount. These realities of practice meant that plaintiff and corporate lawyers generally occupied distinct professional roles, so that one rarely represented the clients of the other.

Although Black was counsel for credit institutions such as the Zurich Insurance Co., he rarely defended corporations in accident cases. He turned down the offer of a partnership in one of the city's leading corporate firms, committing himself to achieving his political and legal ambitions by representing middle- and lower-class clients rather than those from the economic and social elite.

The jury and contingent fee system contributed most to success in a general practice. In accident cases, a lawyer won by tapping community values; and success resulted in a contingent fee, a percentage of the amount the jury awarded the plaintiff. An effective personal-injury attorney was able regularly to convince juries that his client should receive damages, yet in Birmingham, as elsewhere, the law restricted those eligible for jury service to generally respectable, tax-paying, property-holding citizens. Women, blacks, and the poor usually were excluded. The litigants, however, came from all walks of life. Consequently, the successful trial lawyer had to know just what emotions to touch amidst the tangle of hopes, fears, prejudices, sympathies, and interests that respectable jurors shared regarding ethnic, racial, religious, worker, and business groups.

Hugo Black's awareness of the ambiguity inherent in the popular attachment to community respectability and individual independence equipped him for success before Birmingham's juries. On one level this awareness taught simply to avoid "saying things that may leave lasting scars." When "a young lawyer in Birmingham made a personal attack on me I killed him with kindness. The result was a jury verdict for every cent of the damages that I claimed." The "easy way is to attack your opponent with vigor." At a deeper level, however, intense concern for community standing and moralistic education in religion and the classics enabled him to touch jurors' conflicting emotions regarding personal accountability, independence, and dependency. A lawyer "whose career depends to a very large extent on his capacity to persuade" should, he wrote, "possess internal wisdom and goodness" if he seeks to "appeal to exalted ideals" of his "hearers."

Black's sensitivity to the dynamics of persuasion blended opportunism and fundamental convictions about human behavior. He believed that the criminal deserved the best possible defense and that plaintiffs and defendants deserved the ablest representation. Accordingly, like most lawyers Black would subordinate abstract issues of justice to the necessities of winning a case. In so doing he might snatch points from history and the classics—often out of context—in order to support whatever case he needed to make. Expediency alone, however, did not explain Black's frequent use of classical and historical references. His success before juries resulted from a keen understanding of human nature, which he believed was changeless. This presumption led in turn to the conviction that an understanding of human action recorded by historians such as the Roman scholar Tacitus provided guidance for those seeking to convince people in modern times. Black's growing stature as a lawyer only strengthened the conviction that his exploration and application of the past brought rewards in the present.

The case of *Mary Miniard* v. *Illinois Central Railroad* suggested why "wisdom" and the appeal to "ideals" could win. Miniard, a railroad passenger, claimed that the company was guilty of "willful and wanton negligence in allowing a negro woman [who apparently was insane] to abuse her and insult her, and humiliate her." Representing Miniard as plaintiff, Black asked the jury to award damages commensurate with the "humiliation and indignity" she had suffered. Black thus evoked the vague but potent sentiments absorbed in the community's attachment to respectability. He pitted the railroad—the symbol of impersonal, irresponsible power—against a lone, free, and innocent white woman. Since a black woman was the supposed instigator, Black's argument also touched the jury's racial presumptions; but since she was insane, insofar as race was an issue it was almost certainly secondary to the more compelling demand that the railroad be held accountable to the community's standard of conduct and the fact that the railroad had the means to pay damages. Unsurprisingly, Black won.

A case involving a black plaintiff, Willie Morton, indicated the complexity of the attitudes concerning race. Morton, a convict held twenty-two days beyond his prison sentence as a worker for the Sloss Sheffield Steel and Iron Company of Birmingham, turned to Black to win release. This case touched large issues. It was common for counties to lease convicts to private businesses. Lacking an adequate tax base for prisoner support, local governments shifted the costs of food, shelter, and discipline to private enterprise, which in return received cheap labor. A system characterized by considerable brutality, it was repeatedly attacked by Progressives, eventually including Black himself as President of the Alabama Anti-Convict Lease Association. However, since most prisoners were poor blacks, and the populace resisted raising taxes to support a race commonly stigmatized as criminal by nature, the system persisted.

The abuse inherent in the system undermined respect for law and order, which whites counted on to preserve peace within the black community. In addition, white labor groups resisted convict leasing because it created unfair competition with free workers. Moreover, the former convicts, attracted by local industrial jobs, tended to remain in the city after they were freed; and though many whites regarded blacks as inferior, orderly free black employees nonetheless were essential to Birmingham's general welfare. Failure to hold corporations and public officials accountable for clear violations of the law encouraged community instability associated with race and class conflict.

Morton's cause, then, had potential symbolic significance, and it was the first case Black tried in Birmingham's circuit court. As a new attorney he had practiced only in inferior tribunals before the justice of the peace. Circuit court trials were before a jury that could award the plaintiff damages, a percentage of which Black would get if he won. However, counsel for both Morton and the corporation were required to argue the proper pleas. Black had learned the pleading system in law school, but had never before tested his understanding in court. Representing the corporation was William I. Grubb, one of the city's most experienced defense lawyers and a master of pleading. Repeatedly he sought to mislead Black with immaterial pleas, but the young lawyer countered every one effectively. Finally, Judge A.O. Lane, a former mayor of Birmingham, told Grubb "it seems plain you cannot plead this young man out of court, so I suggest you simply join issue and go to trial now." The jury decided in Morton's favor, awarding $137.50 in damages, of which Black and his partner received half.

The *Pryor, Miniard,* and *Morton* cases were typical of hundreds in which Black won jury verdicts for plaintiffs with contingent fees of usually thirty-three percent, amounting to an annual income few Birmingham lawyers could match, totaling about $47,000. In this success Black had learned to adopt the values learned in Clay County to Alabama's leading industrial and population center.

Black owed the start of his public career to the Willie Morton case. Lane, the presiding judge, was deeply involved in the Progressive campaign to establish a commission form of government in Birmingham. In 1910 legislation enabled the city to annex the suburbs, and that shifted the balance of power in favor of evangelical protestants and against the ethnic minorities who controlled the downtown. The next year 123 miners, primarily black convicts, were killed in a mine disaster, a tragedy that enabled Progressives to win support for legislation replacing Birmingham's system of aldermen with a city commission. Hoping to ensure success of the new commission, Progressives sought public officials acceptable to both evangelical and ethnic groups. Lane, who was appointed police commissioner with responsibility for the city's criminal justice system, had the authority to select the inferior court judge who would preside over petty criminal cases involving predominately black defendants. Lane recalled the Birmingham newcomer who had skillfully defended Willie Morton a few years before. He can "fill the bench" well, Lane told the *Age-Herald*.

In 1911 Hugo Black became police court judge. So that the new appointee could continue practicing law, commissioner Lane limited the time the court sat to the early morning hours. Black's pay for the job was only $1,500; he replaced three judges and numerous other officials who had cost Birmingham nearly $33,000 annually. Accordingly, at his first morning court session he announced, there "shall be no delay in the matter of summoning witnesses or conducting trials. I shall require absolute punctuality and the best order." The *Birmingham News* reported that the commission had started off right and the public was delighted.

Each morning from the bench the young judge looked out upon the dregs of a city known for violence—prostitutes, loafers, petty thieves, crapshooters, and drunks. They also included those who the night before had in anger or out of carelessness harmed others with fists, guns, razors, or switchblades. Birmingham's petty criminal court thus confronted directly the tensions inherent in the community's deepest concerns for order, security, and respectability.

Black's handling of the job received considerable public notice. Dubbed by one police reporter as "Hugo to Hell," he nonetheless established a reputation for fairness and effectiveness. On a typical morning he opened the door to the "dingy, dark, and dirty back room in the city hall that is misnamed a courtroom," and braced himself for an "odor that was enough to start the Bubonic plague." He then took off his coat, pulled up his sleeves, and sat down before a crowded room and a docket listing 120 names. He settled every case by noon, and "everyone got a hearing." Black vigorously upheld the vagrancy laws, yet if he thought the facts warranted it, he decided against police officers. In one such case police broke up a dance, arresting twenty-two blacks; but Black released them all, holding that the officers had "no more right to break up that dance than any other." Another time a black defendant admitted shooting craps but denied that a gun found at the game was his. "I am inclined to believe you, and you can go," the judge ruled. As a result, a newspaper reported, when "a nigger succeeds in convincing Judge Black of his innocence despite the testimony of arresting police officers, he is going some."

Black's approach reflected ambivalent community tensions. Annual statistics showed that in one year 59 percent of the city's homicides involved only black defendants and victims, and the percentage in which blacks killed whites was only 4 percent. Actually, whites killed whites in 25 percent of the homicides, but innumerable *Birmingham News* reports agreed with a grand jury that exclaimed in 1909 that the white man's burden was the criminal negro. White law enforcement officers therefore sometimes killed blacks for the slightest reason. In 1910 a policeman shot to death a thirteen-year-old black girl stealing some pieces of coal. The tragedy compelled members of the black Shiloh Baptist Church to publish a resolution imploring whites to remember that the "strength and character of a people are manifested as much in protecting the weak and helpless as in conquering the mighty." In response a small but influential segment of Birmingham's respectable white citizens agreed with a letter appearing in the *Age-Herald,* a newspaper generally representing Progressive opinion and favoring humanitarian causes. The letter deplored the "cruel, brutal, inexcusable murder of Negroes." Anyone "provided he has the money and influence enough, and be not a Negro may with impunity violate any criminal statute, even to the extent of murdering his neighbors." Finally, the letter declared: "We have carried our own, the white people's interest, too far."

The city's police chief, a supporter of the new commission system established in 1911, held similar views. "Everyday I see old broken down negro men and women brought into police court and fined a dollar for some little minor offense. The old darky has not got enough clothes on to make a gum wad; he probably has not enough money to buy a crust of bread, and lives in a little shack somewhere in an alley," the police chief told the *Age-Herald*. "He has to pay his fine and costs from a loan shark who charges him 25 cents on the dollar. The whole thing is wrong," he said. "Such treatment has got to stop."

Such criticism reflected broader opposition to the fee system. The beneficiaries depended on the police judge's frequently fining and imposing lengthy sentences upon those passing through his court. Central to the Progressives' new commission government was an attack on the corrupt bosses who benefited from the fees. Lane undoubtedly appointed Black because he was confident that the young lawyer who had defended poor-black Willie Morton against a powerful corporation would attack the old order with the same determination. As Black meted out expeditious justice, he limited the fines paid, the opportunities for police to appear in court, and the numbers incarcerated in the local jail. In doing so he aligned himself with the *Age-Herald*, Lane, and Birmingham's police chief in advocating some measure of equal justice for everyone, including blacks.

Opposition to the fee system was part of the struggle to wrest control of local government from the "city-hall gang." Lane himself, a popular, two-term, moderate mayor, had won praise from whites and blacks for "fairness and justice." During the 1908 strike, however, he had led a white "citizens' posse" to restore order, decrying not only labor unrest but also the threat of "social equality" the unions posed. Racial concern thus did not extend beyond the typical north Alabama preference for limited equality before the law and customary, rather than state-imposed, segregation. In addition, the Progressives linked their attack on the fee system with the demand for economy in government. Consequently, they advocated strict enforcement of the vagrancy laws.

Judge Black's conduct on the police court reflected these values and interests. He undermined the fee system but faithfully enforced the vagrancy laws. On the whole, his actions were consistent with the economic and political presumptions of Birmingham's Progressives. In his first public office he identified with the political establishment's Progressive activists. Black recognized and enforced the community's conviction that individual accountability and social welfare were interdependent. He perceived and implemented popular sentiments regarding personal conduct and community solidarity.

He soon found himself enmeshed in a much wider controversy. At the very time his judicial proficiency struck at the fee system, *Survey, A Journal of Constructive Philanthropy* began an exhaustive investigation of Birmingham. Identified with national Progressive reform, *Survey* attacked the community's inequitable funding of education favoring whites over blacks. The magazine also criticized the deplorable working conditions imposed upon women and children in former Progressive Governor B. B. Comer's mill known as "Hell's Half Acre," but above all *Survey* exposed the evils of the fee system. It revealed a county sheriff whose exploitive practices reputably earned him $80,000 annually, including the sums designated for the prisoners' meals. "When a state fee system steals a man's liberty, it steals about all he has," the journal exclaimed, "but when officials go beyond that and take most of his food allowance, they have stripped him bare indeed."

National media attention prompted local reaction. Eight weeks after *Survey* published its Birmingham expose, a federal grand jury condemned the county's criminal justice system as "damnable," "highway robbery," and "extortion." The federal judge receiving the report was W. I. Grubb, the corporate lawyer against whom Black had successfully argued in the Willie Morton case. Grubb accepted the grand jury's observation that the fee system victimized poor blacks. The grand jury called for federal intervention and the "giant shadow of the U.S. government standing by with far-reaching arms and a grim determination to at least brook no violation of its statutes." Federal power, however, was limited. State and local action was essential in order to strike at the root of the problem by paying Jefferson County's 150 justices of the peace, 150 constables, and numerous deputy sheriffs a regular salary. Although the program required increased taxes, a coalition of prominent Birmingham professional, real estate, utility, industrial, commercial, and banking leaders, with labor support, organized a campaign resulting in passage of a constitutional amendment establishing state rather than local funding of county law enforcement officials' salaries.

Black now saw the opportunity to win election to higher office. During the fall of 1912, he resigned his judgeship and prepared to run for county prosecutor. He confronted a divided public in which downtown, predominately ethnic groups opposed suburban, evangelical protestants, most of them prohibitionists who attacked the fee system because agents paid by law enforcement officials used liquor and craps to entice innocent black workers to engage in immoral conduct. Liquor posed a threat because it fostered "Deep, Dark, Damnable Dens of Degradation" where "vice is flagrant and where evil doers hide and congregate to hatch iniquity." In 1913 moral white citizens were horrified when a grand jury discovered in such a place that "while the filthy shacks" were "supposed to be exclusively for whites, evidence of colored men having visited white women has been obtained." Respectable citizens knew, then, that liquor and gambling created the "menace of the liquor filled negro."

These tensions led Black to campaign as the enemy of gambling. But since other, better known, candidates could also tap evangelical concern, he had to make a broader appeal. He stood for "helpless people confronting the power of the big absentee corporations that dominated their lives." His preference for defending individuals sustained the claim that his people were "plain folks," not a "few capitalists or a ring of politicians." This strategy attracted downtown ethnic voters as well as those employed in the mills and mines, in an attempt to garner the votes of groups who otherwise opposed one another.

Like the Clay County Populists, he styled himself the underdog. Pursuing an intensely personal, face-to-face campaign in an old car, he visited every section of Jefferson County, often several times. Numerous contacts cultivated since arriving in Birmingham proved valuable. Day and night he went where he could see people, to lodges, picnics, basket suppers, stores, baseball games, giving practically every minute of his time to the campaign except that devoted to his law practice. Black won the endorsement of influential people among the poor, the middling ranks, and the well-to-do, including commissioner Lane and federal judge Grubb.

His principal opponent was the incumbent county prosecutor, a member of one of Alabama's most prominent political families, Harrington P. Heflin. Daily, Black's supporters flooded Jefferson County with slips of paper posing the question: "Heflin or Black?" Finally, during the fall of 1914, to the surprise of the political establishment Jefferson County elected Black to a four-year term as county prosecutor. The Populist-style campaign had attracted rural and suburban prohibitionists, as well as diverse ethnic voters. The triumph, Black wrote, was the "result of hard, concentrated work, not only during eight and a half months of active campaigning but during" seven years in Birmingham.

Black entered the prosecutor's office in early 1915, just as Progressivism began to decline. Alabamians elevated to the Senate Oscar W. Underwood, a loyal Democratic congressman from Birmingham, who only tacitly approved President Woodrow Wilson's Progressive policies and opposed statewide prohibition. Of more concern to Black, the state's governor immediately appointed the defeated Heflin as one of Birmingham's criminal court judges. The new prosecutor would now often have to argue cases before Judge Heflin, the very individual he had campaigned against as a member of the old "courthouse ring."

For months prior to passage of the constitutional amendment establishing state funding of criminal justice salaries, Black attacked the fee system. Finding the jails jammed and over 3,268 cases awaiting trial, he released more than 500 petty offenders, claiming they had been helplessly entrapped by a corrupt system. At the same time, Black vigorously prosecuted genuine violations of the law. Jefferson County supported his stand, favoring the amendment by a vote of nearly eight to one.

Nevertheless, the "murder capital of the world" presented the young prosecutor with many serious criminal cases. In one coal mining area of the county called the "bloody beat," whites often murdered blacks. Shortly after Black warned against the killings, two brothers killed a black man, then burned the body on a pyre. When Black prosecuted the brothers, the jury convicted and sentenced them to be hanged. Even though he won many such verdicts, juries sometimes allowed racial presumptions to prevail. Thus, despite the prosecutor's plea that a policeman's cold-blooded murder of a black teenager warranted the death penalty, the jury convicted him only of second-degree murder, which carried a sentence of twenty-five years. Moreover, Judge Heflin frequently permitted delays in controversial suits, so much so that Black got the Alabama Supreme Court to assign extra judges to Jefferson County to expedite the case load.

True to his campaign promises, he also defended workers against powerful corporate interests. Black successfully prosecuted coal companies for wage practices which were unfair to miners and pressured insurance companies to comply with laws protecting the insurance settlements of injured workers. Black even initiated a grand jury investigation of one local community's ruthless police interrogation methods, reportedly "so cruel" that they would "bring discredit and shame upon the most uncivilized and barbarous community." Late at night Bessemer police would tie to a doorknob black prisoners arrested on vague suspicion and beat them until they confessed. The grand jury report, in words reputedly written by Black, exclaimed: "A man does not forfeit his right to be treated as a human being by reason of the fact that he is charged with, or an officer suspects that he is guilty of a crime." The Bessemer investigation had little long-term impact and the controversy quickly died down. Nevertheless, it revealed Black's values. Employing classical rhetorical terms he attacked the Bessemer officials' arbitrariness not only as "tyrannical and despotic," but as "dishonorable," and "rights must not be surrendered to any officer or set of officers, so long as human life is held sacred, and human liberty and human safety of paramount importance."

Black also appealed directly to influential evangelical protestants in his attack on liquor. In 1915 the legislature made prohibition the law of the state, whereupon the *Alabama Christian Advocate* rejoiced that "Liquor domination in Alabama is a thing of the past, thanks be to God." Within two years Birmingham's suburban evangelicals had taken over the city commission, defeating the downtown, anti-prohibition ethnic groups. Consequently, although the Progressives' influence was otherwise waning, a policy central to their cause and constituency now dominated city government. As county prosecutor, Black was responsible for enforcing the new order, and there was much for him to do. Bootleggers, connected with brewery interests, set up "blind tigers" often indistinguishable from the craps dives. Moreover, newspaper interests, faced with declining revenues from the loss of lucrative liquor advertisements, suddenly perceived a profound threat to freedom of the press.

On these issues, Black subordinated individual rights to community control. Claiming that state interference with liquor advertisement violated the First Amendment, a Birmingham newsstand operator continued to sell publications with liquor ads. The county prosecutor sought from Heflin's city court an injunction prohibiting the action, but the judge refused, favoring the First Amendment protection. On appeal to the Alabama Supreme Court, however, Black triumphed. In another case Black challenged brewery interests seeking to circumvent prohibition by producing "near beer," a substance they claimed was not alcohol within the meaning of the state law. Judge

Grubb rejected the argument that the prohibition law violated individual rights protected under the due process clause of the Fourteenth Amendment; again Black won.

Eventually such victories attracted the attention of the attorney general in Montgomery. State officials caught six whiskey bootleggers in Girard, Alabama, seizing $600,000 worth of liquor. The attorney general appointed Black as special state prosecutor to try the "Girard Six," but when they failed to present themselves in court he ordered the destruction of the confiscated alcohol. The act aroused immediate protest from the bootleggers and their influential supporters, who argued that the state had unlawfully destroyed private property. Black retorted that the defendants had forfeited their rights when they did not appear for trial. Newspapers statewide supported this view, proclaiming that Black was "the man of the hour in these events." Eventually the case reached the Alabama Supreme Court, and once more the decision was in Black's favor.

Another development, however, had more ominous implications. In 1916 the Ku Klux Klan established Alabama's first klavern in Birmingham. Amidst the growing tension arising from the war in Europe, the Klan condemned Catholics, Jews, blacks, foreigners, strikers, bootleggers, immoral women, and other such sinners. It drew members from the same evangelical protestants who supported prohibition and opposed ethnic minorities. During the same year, nightriders burned a Catholic church not far from Birmingham. The city's klavern actually grew out of a secret anti-Catholic organization called the True Americans, started by the pastor of the First Baptist Church. By the 1917 election for commission president, these rabidly anti-ethnic elements had so divided the community that even many evangelical protestants resisted them. Nevertheless, the victor in the election had been endorsed by the True Americans, and upon taking office he replaced the Catholic sheriff with a Klan member. Although Black belonged to the same church as the True Americans' founder, and members of his Sunday class were Klansmen, he was affiliated with neither group.

As the United States was about to go to war, Black confronted a more direct challenge. For over two years he had effectively prosecuted powerful interests in Birmingham. By early 1917 his courthouse conflict with the Heflin group reached an impasse, paralleling the community's wider ethnic and political struggles. Finally, Black's opponents exploited an ambiguity in Alabama's constitution concerning the county treasurer's responsibility for the salaries paid the prosecutor's assistants. Since the treasurer was aligned with Heflin's faction, the controversy threatened Black's ability to control his own staff. After considerable litigation resulting in two appeals to the state supreme court, the decision went against Black. As a result he resigned, and shortly after the United States entered World War I he joined the army.

Shaping his decision was a profound dilemma. Unlike Grubb and Heflin, Black had the direct support of neither Birmingham's social elite nor the city's bosses. To gain and maintain power he had to appeal to individual interests who generally opposed one another. As plaintiff's lawyer and elected official he ameliorated divisive social and political tension, successfully accommodating the community and individual values inherent in the popular commitment to respectability. His attack on the fee system and defense of distressed plaintiffs or criminal defendants showed that community unity and individual rights were, to a point, at least, interdependent, but Black's enforcement of prohibition and the preference for the new suburban, evangelical protestant majority it represented undercut this balance. The resulting conflict left him vulnerable to the same factional struggles that had overwhelmed the Progressives; the growing involvement of the Ku Klux Klan in the prohibition crusade revealed just how intractable the confrontation had become.

Black sought escape from such uncertainty by going to war. Initially he had agreed with President Wilson's secretary of state, William Jennings Bryan, who argued that the terrible European struggle had resulted from immoral, profit-hungry munitions manufacturers. Once Congress declared war, however, Black's precarious political situation eased the decision to defend his country. He became an army captain but served without leaving the United States; and after the Armistice, with honorable discharge in hand, he took the train to Birmingham early in 1919 to resume law practice and confront an unpredictable peace.

CHAPTER THREE

The Perils of Prejudice (1919–1929)

❖
❖

Hugo Black's return to Birmingham in 1919 was not auspicious. The *Age-Herald* reported briefly that "Captain Black has resumed practice and has opened his office on the ninth floor of the First National Bank Building," and nothing suggested that the relatively short absence from the bar had diminished his ability to attract clients. Unexpected developments made it essential that his practice become profitable immediately. During his military service Black consistently spent beyond his means, drawing repeatedly upon his modest savings and investment income managed by his friend, the merchant Herman M. Beck. He also contributed collateral to finance a speculative merger between two Birmingham banks and lost everything when the merger collapsed. A short time later a severe case of pneumonia almost killed him. Although friends provided care and moral support during the recovery, Black had to borrow from his brother's widow to pay medical bills.

He therefore began the 1920s with some anxiety. Passage of the Eighteenth Amendment and the triumph of prohibition compounded the uncertainty. Black's career as a plaintiff's lawyer, police court judge, and county prosecutor had taught him the strengths and the weaknesses arising from the popular attachment to respectability, community unity, and individual rights, entwined with the evangelical Protestants' support for prohibition and the emergence of the Ku Klux Klan. After the war this background made Black especially sensitive to the dramatic rise of the Klan. The Invisible Empire in Alabama and elsewhere remained committed to terrorizing ethnic and racial minorities, although it publicly downplayed these tactics in an effort to attract middle-class members. Many respectable Alabamians took the oath of loyalty, which in turn created a broad-based organization with considerable political clout. Black could ignore these developments only at his peril.

Within months after the return to Birmingham, Black began displaying his talent for winning damage settlements in personal injury cases. The lucrative contingent fees he received enabled him not only to pay his debts but also to purchase a new car with cash. He renewed his involvement in numerous fraternal and civic organizations as well, including the Masons, the Knights of Pythias, the Birmingham Chamber of Commerce, and the American Legion. In 1920 the city's Bar Association elected him to serve on the executive committee. In addition, Black continued reading all of Thomas Jefferson's published writings, other historical works, and various Greek and Roman classics. He also remained a fervent tennis player and remained active in the First Baptist Church and taught Sunday school.

Black encountered a community absorbed in conflict. Postwar Birmingham possessed wide, straight streets, a rising skyline that included the South's tallest building, and a growing population. But promoters' dreams of replacing Atlanta or New Orleans as the South's leading city remained unfulfilled. Industrial diversification, which fostered economic prominence, was also a source of tension. The Pittsburgh-based United States Steel parent firm imposed on its Birmingham subsidiary a discriminatory pricing policy that offset the advantage Birmingham should have had from lower labor costs. Increased population exacerbated the competition between whites and blacks for jobs; and wartime federal regulation failed to provide union recognition. When the United Mine Workers renewed the struggle lost in 1908, public officials used force and appeals to white supremacy to defeat the union, charging it "with a history of associating the black man on terms of perfect equality with the white man." In the new struggle, moreover, the authorities had a new ally—the Ku Klux Klan.

Black knew many who secretly belonged to the Invisible Empire. The Klan's virulent anti-Catholicism and its affiliation with the Anti-Saloon League's successful prohibition crusade had inevitably enmeshed the Klan in politics. During the closely contested U.S. Senate race of 1920, it opposed the incumbent Oscar W. Underwood. Although Underwood won, his victory was narrow enough that Black realized that a Klan-prohibitionist alliance could have a profound impact on the state's political future.

Black pondered the possible effects on his own future. His reputation as plaintiff's lawer was confirmed when the Alabama Supreme Court repeatedly sustained large damage awards in personal injury cases. Before long his was among the highest income of any attorneys in the city. He began thinking seriously about marriage. Black was thirty-four, but his slender, athletic build, quick, assertive actions, and outgoing friendliness suggested a man of much younger age. During a dance at the exclusive Southern Club he met Josephine Foster, whom he began to court with the same determination that had led to his legal and political achievements.

Josephine Foster was as attractive, intelligent, and independent as her family was eminently respectable and socially prominent. She had completed her education at Sweet Briar College. Caught up in the enthusiasm of Wilsonian idealism during the war, she joined the navy's female branch, the Yeomanettes. Her father, Sterling Foster, was the son of one of Alabama's established black-belt planter families. Josephine's mother, Ann Patterson, belonged to a leading Tennessee family. Josephine's parents had no concern about Black's family roots, but they did wonder about his reputation as a labor lawyer. Only partially in jest did they call Josephine's determined suitor "that young Bolshevik." Moreover, their daughter was about thirteen years younger than he. But ultimately parental reservations dissolved and Hugo and Josephine were married at the Fosters' home in a private family ceremony on February 23, 1921.

Marriage completed Black's rise into Birmingham's elite. In their home Josephine acquainted Black with classical music and other cultural refinements. There also their two sons, Hugo La Fayette, Jr., and Sterling Foster, were born. Membership in the Birmingham Country Club and Junior League reflected the family's social stature and prosperity.

Black kept in touch, however, with his many relatives in Clay County. A letter to an eighteen-year-old niece explained that two things counted more than almost everything else in this life—work and endurance. He also stressed the value of exercise and concluded with a dearly won insight: "There is a predisposition on the part of many of our family to become moody, despondent, cynical, unduly critical of others, and pessimistic. That is an excellent thing to avoid. Optimism brings more happiness and makes more friends and gets more of anything it goes after."

A comfortable, gracious private life and secure professional stature did not dull Black's political ambition. Increasingly he considered the possibility of running for the Senate in 1926. Several factors suggested that he might have a chance. Passage of the Seventeenth Amendment in 1913 replaced state legislatures with direct popular vote as the means of electing senators, and that weakened the influence of the bosses. The Nineteenth Amendment, enfranchising women, had a similar impact. In addition, Alabama had altered its Democratic primary system: if no candidate won a clear majority, the one receiving the highest number of first- and second-place votes was declared the winner. These changes diffused the support candidates might garner primarily because they were well known, socially prominent, or the candidates of the political establishment. Moreover, the prohibition issue and the growing influence of the Klan undercut traditional political alignments.

In the early 1920s voters throughout Alabama began to encounter Hugo Black's name. Mobile, the state's leading port and a city with a large Catholic population and strong Latin traditions, was an illegal liquor center. In 1923 federal authorities indicted 117 leading Mobilians for violation of national prohibition laws, including the chief of police, a county commissioner, and a wealthy businessman who eventually represented the city in the U.S. Congress. Republican U.S. Attorney General Harlan Fiske Stone appointed Black special prosecutor in the case. After months of proceedings—reported daily as front page news across the state—the police chief and several others were convicted. As president of the Alabama Prison Reform Association, Black also led the fight to abolish the state's infamous convict-lease system. This evil, he wrote the Governor, permitted corporate exploitation by striking at "the wage scale of the free miner." The well-publicized campaign finally triumphed in 1927.

Black's victory in another controversial case attracted still more public attention. Henry Lewis, an illiterate, indigent convict working under the lease system, was seriously injured in a mining accident because of the company's negligence. A jury in the state court awarded Lewis $4000 damages, but before paying the company filed for bankruptcy. In order to win recovery Black removed the case to federal court, arguing for Lewis's claim against the company's estate under federal bankruptcy law. The federal judge ruled, however, that federal law protected only creditors having valid contracts, and the convict Lewis had no such contract. Black then asked the U.S. Supreme Court to accept the case *in forma pauperis,* permission given to a poor person to appeal without liability for costs. In *Lewis* v. *Roberts* (1925) the Court unanimously reversed the lower tribunal's decision. The decision publicized both a good cause and Black's leadership in it.

But Black's role in a nationally reported, sensational murder trial was more problematic. Edwin R. Stephenson, a Protestant pastor of uncertain official standing, shot and killed Father James E. Coyle in broad daylight on the front porch of Coyle's rectory, not far from the Birmingham courthouse. After shooting the unarmed Coyle, Stephenson turned himself in and confessed to the city's police chief. He said that earlier the same day Coyle had performed a marriage ceremony between Stephenson's eighteen-year-old daughter, Ruth, and a middle-aged Puerto Rican paper hanger, Pedro Gussman. Stephenson claimed that he went to the rectory in search of his daughter but encountered Coyle instead. Because he had called Coyle "a dirty dog," he attested, the priest struck him, whereupon Stephenson fired his revolver. Coyle was the leader of Birmingham's Catholic community, which included twelve churches. Coinciding with the Klan's continuing terrorist campaign against ethnic and racial minorities, the murder aroused passions in Birmingham and throughout Alabama.

Stephenson's lawyer was Hugo Black, who used all his skill to touch the jury's deepest sentiments. During one dramatic moment he called Gussman to appear in court. "I just wanted the jury to see this man," he said, and the *Birmingham News* reported that the "lights were arranged in the courtroom so that the darkness of Gussman's complexion would be accentuated." Then, during the summation, Black characterized two witnesses to the murder, who were Catholics, as "brothers in falsehood as well as faith." He said further that, since most of Puerto Rico's population were mulatto descendants of Negroes, if Gussman claimed to be of Spanish origin, he had "descended a long way." But he saved until last the most powerful appeals to fear and prejudice. "Because a man becomes a priest does not mean he is divine. He has no more right to protection than a Protestant minister. Who believes Ruth Stephenson has not been proselytized? A child of a Methodist does not suddenly depart from her religion unless someone has planted in her mind the seeds of influence," Black exclaimed in his summation. "If the eyes of the world are upon the verdict of this jury, I would write that verdict in words that cannot be misunderstood, that the homes of Birmingham cannot be touched. If that brings disgrace," he concluded, "God hasten the disgrace." The jury acquitted Stephenson. And although critics nationwide and within Alabama condemned Black's tactics, considerable public opinion throughout the state supported the verdict and the man who won it.

Meanwhile, Black's political strategy confronted a real dilemma. New constitutional and legal voting standards established an environment weakening traditional political alignments. Since Black remained a political outsider, however, victory in a statewide race depended on his ability to win the support of diverse groups, which usually opposed one another. Both labor and business supported the end of convict leasing: one to reduce unfair job competition, the other because the system hurt productive efficiency. However, Black's reputation as a "young Bolshevik" alienated many business interests. On the other hand, defenders of the old Progressivism no doubt applauded his fight for the destitute in *Lewis* v. *Roberts*, a stand not without risks, in light of the increasingly explosive role of ethnic and racial prejudice in politics. Black could also count on the support of numerous fraternal organizations, but social and cultural tensions divided these organizations as well. Some, like the Knights of Pythias, welcomed as members and leaders Jews such as Beck, whereas other orders such as the Masons were havens for Klansmen.

As a lawyer and politician Black had attempted to overcome these tensions by tapping the ambiguous yet potent popular commitment to respectability. He often won by convincing jurors and voters that community unity and individual rights were interdependent. The Mobile prohibition prosecution and Stephenson case suggested how far he was willing to go to embrace community ideals and fears. His enforcement of prohibition laws evidenced the influence of the evangelical Protestants who believed that independence and community stability depended on responsible individual behavior achieved by eradication of liquor. The Mobile case thus demonstrated that rich and powerful special interests were being held accountable to community standards. Black's defense of Stephenson suggested, however, the equivocal character of appeals to respectability. Since community solidarity required that the family remain inviolate, Father Coyle's blessing of the marriage between Ruth Stephenson and Gussman aroused the jury's profoundest emotions. The sensational murder trial was perhaps most significant because it preceded Black's affiliation with the Invisible Empire. He probably knew that members of the jury, as well as the chief of police testifying on Stephenson's behalf, were Klansmen. Indeed, years later a Klan leader, present at the notorious trial, quipped: "Hugo didn't have much trouble winning that verdict." By the mid-1920s, as his preparation for a statewide political campaign progressed, his Klan involvement deepened. A friend, the son of one of his former school teachers in Clay County, was an official in the Birmingham Klavern; the pastor of his church and some of his Sunday school pupils were members; various fraternal brothers had donned the white robes; and many of his clients came from the same class that made up the Klan's rank and file. Finally, his contact with the Klan was inseparable from his defense of prohibition, for it was hard to tell where the Anti-Saloon "League ends and the Klan begins."

Thus in 1923 he joined the Ku Klux Klan. As the organization's influence grew after the war, its clandestine whippings, burnings, and attacks upon innocent people increased—despite the Klan's public disavowals of violence. Racial and ethnic tensions linked to job competition among blacks, Catholics, and white Protestant workers, and the ambivalent attachment to individual rights and community solidarity reflected by the prohibition crusade, encouraged the Klan's dramatic growth. Most new members, particularly the professionals, were not interested in violence; they yearned instead for reassurance and security in face of the uncertainties of the 1920s. Black's livelihood as a plaintiff's lawyer depended on a keen sensitivity to these sentiments. Lacking the support of the elite and the bosses, his election to statewide office was unlikely without Klan affiliation. As a result, although he condemned the violence, he nonetheless took the oath of eternal loyalty to the Invisible Empire.

Moreover, although Black felt no prejudice toward individual Catholics, he profoundly distrusted the Church. He resented the fact that rental property owned by the Church was not taxed; most of its revenue came from the poor and not enough was being returned. Black's success as a trial lawyer also hinged on the Klan. Years later in a confidential interview, Black explained, "I was trying a lot of cases against corporations, jury cases, and I found out that all the corporation lawyers were in the Klan. . . . A lot of the jurors were too so I figured I'd better be even-up." In the Stephenson case, the community's fears and prejudices converged with his own antipathies, political ambitions, and livelihood as a lawyer, encouraging the decision to join the organization that threatened the very social order he otherwise defended.

Oscar Underwood's eroding political fortunes convinced Black to run for the Senate. Underwood sought the Democratic presidential nomination in 1924, but success depended on overcoming a pronounced national party split. One side included ethnic, immigrant, industrial, and urban groups represented by Catholic Al Smith; on the other side was the solid South, which stood for native white Protestants, prohibition, agriculture, the Ku Klux Klan, and racial segregation. Underestimating his ability to hold Dixie, Underwood took a compromising position on prohibition, but above all he vigorously condemned the Invisible Empire. The stand undoubtedly cost him the nomination. As one Alabama delegate to the Democratic convention regretfully observed, "Oscar won't demagogue, not even a little." Returning to Alabama after the Republican presidential victory, Underwood realized that the likelihood of winning the Senate race in 1926 was slim. As a result, on July 1, 1925, "Democracy's Peerless Leader" announced he would not seek reelection, and then left the state to retire near the nation's capital.

Black was among those who sought to succeed Underwood. The leading candidates, however, were former governor Thomas E. Kilby and John H. Bankhead, Jr., a member of one of Alabama's foremost political families. Both men were millionaires involved in corporate enterprise, but Kilby had a record as a pro-business progressive who was also bone dry and adamantly anti-Catholic. Bankhead relied primarily on his family's social prominence and association with the state's political establishment. Nevertheless, not long after Underwood's retirement Black returned to Clay County to begin a formal campaign that had been a long time in the planning. Most political observers discounted Black's chances. Even Josephine was certain he could not win. Black started the race much as he had the run for Birmingham County prosecutor: as an outsider and underdog underestimated by nearly everyone but himself and a few close supporters.

Political divisions among the opposition worked to Black's advantage. Kilby appealed to the evangelical Protestant advocates of prohibition, but as governor he had forcibly suppressed labor unrest, thereby alienating a major segment of that group. Bankhead's social stature made him vulnerable to criticism that he was the candidate of the rich and privileged. Moreover, he favored turning Muscle Shoals, one of Alabama's most valuable economic resources, over to private developers and the Alabama Power Company. In addition, though neither Kilby nor Bankhead was a Klan member, they nonetheless voiced sympathy for the Klan's cause, and Bankhead even called the Invisible Empire a patriotic organization. Nevertheless, given a choice Klansmen would likely vote for one they considered their own.

Black exploited these divisions. He pursued a statewide, face-to-face campaign. Black wore out two automobiles on the state's rutted dirt roads, visiting each of Alabama's sixty-seven counties at least twice. He reinforced his reputation as a defender of prohibition in speeches exclaiming: "There is one little saloon that every man can close, and that is the one that is under his nose." In addition, he did not hesitate to tap the fear of Catholic immigrants entwined in the prohibition crusade. "The melting pot idea," he warned, "is dangerous to our national inheritance." He turned his opponents' advantages of wealth and social status, as well as their affiliation with corporate big business, against them. Black believed that Bankhead was the most serious opponent, so he stressed the Alabama Power Company's interest in Muscle Shoals. Evoking his own Clay County family roots, he also asked new women voters in rural areas to help him defeat the notion "that only the rich and powerful sons of the great can serve their state."

He also handled astutely his Klan affiliation. Days after Underwood's retirement he wrote privately to the secretary of the Birmingham klavern, resigning. Black had kept his Klan connection a secret and now he withdrew quietly. Consistently with the organization's avowed political noninvolvement, Alabama Klan leaders did not allow their followers seeking elected office to campaign formally as Klansman. Instead, the Invisible

Empire transmitted its political preferences privately among the faithful. Black's hope for victory depended on appealing to a wide spectrum of voters, including Jews and Catholics. To avoid risking such support, it was essential that Black could, if asked, truthfully deny direct KKK association. Consequently, the Grand Dragon reportedly told him: "Give me a letter of resignation, and I'll keep it in my safe against the day when you'll need to say you're not a Klan member." Thus as long as he retained the leadership's good will, Black received Klan support, while he could nonetheless publicly disclaim membership. He had also provided, however, indisputable written evidence that the Klan could use against him should he ever fall from grace.

Because of the divided field, Black won the 1926 primary. He received a majority of the first- and second-place votes, while Bankhead came in second, and Kilby was last. Yet he received only 32 percent of the total vote. The Montgomery *Advertiser* explained: most Alabamians did not "regard Mr. Black as the most suitable man to succeed the Great Underwood and they voted against him, only they divided their votes." Since all the candidates appealed to the same Democratic voters, including Klansmen, Black (the "darling of the Klan") was "the beneficiary of divided allegiance." Indeed, his 84,877 total votes came remarkably close to the estimated membership of Alabama's Ku Klux Klan in 1926.

Thus Black undoubtedly spoke the truth when shortly after the primary triumph he told an assemblage of Klansmen: "I know that without the support of the members of this organization I would not have been called, even by my enemies, the 'Junior Senator from Alabama.' I realize that I was elected by men who believe in the principles that I have sought to advocate and which are the principles of this organization." As a result he sought to "impress upon" them as "representative of the real Anglo-Saxon sentiment that must and will control the destinies of the stars and stripes," that "I thank you." Then he concluded with the same sort of exclamatory appeal to basic popular values that he had made in the Stephenson case. Black thanked his white-robed brothers with "love," "faith," "trust," and "undying prayer that this great organization will carry on sacredly, true to the real principles of American manhood and womanhood, revering the virtue of the mother of the race, loving the pride of Anglo-Saxon spirit—and I love it—true to the heaven born principles of liberty which were written in the Constitution." The Klan stenographer typing the speech noted, "Great applause." In public Black applied his rhetorical skills on behalf of the anti-liquor crusade while privately he used them to cultivate the Invisible Empire.

Black easily won the fall general election, whereupon he, Josephine, and their two boys moved to Washington. The new Congress did not come into existence until the spring of 1927, and the legislative session did not actually begin until the end of that year. Black used the time to broaden his reading. Shortly after arriving in Washington, he came across and saved an article from *American Magazine* by Will Durant entitled "One Hundred Best Books." Black began reading through Durant's list, gradually building up an extensive personal library of Greek, Roman, European, and American history books. A methodical system of marking and indexing permitted him to return time and again to the insights he found. In addition, he often underlined and made marginal notations in the books. For years he had studied Jefferson and Gibbon. Now he extended his interests to include Adam Smith, Alexander Hamilton, John Adams, John Locke, J. S. Mill, Karl Marx, Aristotle, St. Thomas Aquinas, St. Augustine, Thucydides, Herodotus, Plato, Plutarch, Seneca, Cicero, Virgil, Shakespeare, and Milton. Although his choices of the new reading were indiscriminate, the extent of his markings in each volume confirms how seriously he took what he read. The annotations also suggested the degree to which the reading reinforced the assumption developed during years of politics and successful trial practice that throughout history human nature did not change.

By the time Black and the Senate began deliberations, Alabama politics were again shifting. The Klan's terrorism had degenerated into private vendettas, jeopardizing its support among respectable citizens. Before long the organization's membership in Alabama had dropped by nearly 90 percent. As a result, some state politicians who had won election with Klan support publicly resigned, espousing a new concern for law and order. Although the dissension stimulated a resurgence of the state's traditional Democratic party leadership, the candidacy of Al Smith for the 1928 presidential nomination engendered further controversy. Alabama's bosses did not want to support a Catholic opponent of prohibition, but neither did they want to risk a local revival of the Republican party. Hence, the state's establishment had little choice but to support Smith by appeals to white supremacy. "God meant Alabama to be a white man's state," exclaimed loyal Democrats, "and the Democratic party has been his instrument in keeping it a white man's state." Black delegates had helped to nominate Hoover, whereas "no nigger helped nominate Al Smith." Republicans countered with their own racist appeals, condemning Smith as a "Negro bootlicker." For the first time since reconstruction such slogans helped give a Republican presidential candidate victory in five southern states. But not in Alabama. By a narrow margin the state's black belt placed white supremacy over anti-Catholicism and prohibition, carrying the state for Smith.

During the struggle Black changed ground. Alabama's senior senator, Tom Heflin, proclaimed adamantly, "So help me God, I will vote against Al Smith if they read me out of the Democratic party and drive me from every Senate Committee!" Black, however, withheld comment as long as possible, despite newspaper queries such as "Why do we not hear from Hugo Black in this campaign?" Finally, Black responded that, except for Smith's defense of immigration, his platform was "a clarion call to progressive democracy." The junior senator then cautioned against creating "a noisy division of wets and drys, submerging party issues of Jeffersonian Progress and equal opportunity as opposed to Hamiltonian reaction and special privilege." About the Ku Klux Klan he said nothing at all. Black, who two years before won election because of Klan and prohibitionist support, now aligned himself with the establishment against those same forces.

Black's backing of Smith reflected a sensitivity to political pressures within the Senate. By 1928 the two parties were closely divided in the chamber; and several maverick Republicans, including George Norris of Nebraska, Hiram Johnson of California, and William E. Borah of Idaho, often voted with the Democrats. In an environment in which every vote counted, Black's influence would grow if he remained among the Senate's Democratic faithful. Thus, he parted ways with Heflin. When a Democratic colleague suggested that his reputed Klan support in 1926 made his loyalty in the presidential race questionable, Black snapped back: "That is absolutely untrue. I got all the Ku Klux votes I could get" and "all the Catholic votes I could get, and all the Jew votes I could get, and all the Baptist votes I could get, and all the others, and I have no apology to make for it, and I am here representing them." On ethnic and racial issues Black went along with Heflin, favoring immigration restriction, supporting prohibition, and opposing federal funds for black Howard University. On other policy matters, however, he joined Democrats and the few independent Republicans in vigorous support of what he called progressive democracy.

Party loyalty brought increased power and standing in the Senate. Despite his freshman status, Black became one of Norris's most vocal allies in the struggle to establish a federal electric power project at Muscle Shoals. Senate leaders selected Black to conduct highly publicized investigations of the "power trust" and the "shipping trust." Appointed to the prestigious Foreign Relations Committee, he voted to withdraw the Marines from Nicaragua, for the Kellogg-Briand peace pact, and for Philippine independence. Black also fought for legislation requiring public registration of lobbyists "employed by powerful interests and combinations intent upon special privilege, public pillage, and public plunder." When one such lobbyist suggested that the bill's supporters had communist affiliations, Black exclaimed to a *New York Times* reporter (his former Klan membership conveniently forgotten): "Men and groups who work behind a mask deserve no sympathy and quarter. They are enemies of true government or they would not fear public knowledge."

By the fall of 1929 Black had become a critic of the Hoover administration. His growing influence reflected his ability to judge perceptively the dynamics of power within the Senate and to accommodate these to the changing political realities in Alabama. In the name of party loyalty he left behind the Klan and retreated from prohibition, embracing the very political establishment he had often opposed. Underlying the shifts, however, was a consistent struggle to strike a balance between community interests and individual rights. The effort to balance these values put him increasingly at odds with Hoover's policies; and after the stock market crash of Black Thursday, October 24, this conflict became ever more intractable.

CHAPTER FOUR

The Great Depression and New Deal Liberalism (1929–1937)

❖
❖

As Black confronted the Great Depression his youthful appearance did not suggest a man in his mid-forties. Effective handling of politics in the Senate and back home reflected maturity in adapting long-held beliefs to tumultuous conditions. He blended the insights gleaned from self-education and the experiences of life into a coherent vision based on Jeffersonian democracy, the changelessness of human nature, and an abiding faith in respectability and the interdependency of individual and community welfare. The Depression reaffirmed for Black the fundamental truth of these values and the vital need to reshape them to meet the unprecedented national emergency.

Although the scale of the collapse varied somewhat throughout the nation, Black agreed with sociologists Robert and Helen Merrell Lynd that all Americans faced an economic and a spiritual crisis. It was, they wrote, "a catastrophe involving not only people's values" but also "their very existence." The "great knife of the depression had cut down impartially through the entire population, cleaving open the lives and hopes of rich as well as poor. The experience had been more nearly universal than any prolonged recent emotional experience," approaching in its "elemental shock the primary experiences of birth and death."

Hoover had expected that underwriting big corporations and large farmers with federal credit would stimulate increased prices and profits, which would in turn foster higher employment. He relied on voluntary cooperation between the federal government and industrial and agricultural producers, but fundamental competitive pressures ensured the failure of his hopes. Hoover had refused to enhance the worker's purchasing power—and therefore market demand—either by supporting organized labor or by providing employment through federally funded public works. Finally, his adamant opposition to any federal welfare aid and the states' insufficient provision for such assistance destroyed people's morale, creating profound tensions among individuals and within families. Moreover, in the face of new racial injustice, blacks unavailingly renewed the demand for federal anti-lynching legislation.

Conditions in Birmingham drove home for Black the extent to which the Depression threatened people's material and psychological welfare. Following the stock market crash 25,000 of Birmingham's 108,000 wage earners were unemployed, and many of the remainder worked only reduced hours. Prior to Black Thursday, the city's Community Chest had provided food for 800 families, primarily during the winter. As the Depression deepened, it had to find the means to assist 9000 families throughout the entire year. Men yearned for work. When the city announced a few openings for individuals to clean the parks at $2 a day, there were 12,712 applications. Fertilizer sales fell 72 percent, automobile purchases dropped 85 percent. Hoping to exploit the disruption of community stability and the values upon which it rested, the Communist party became active in Birmingham in 1930.

Ideas cultivated through intense personal study shaped Black's perceptions. Interspersed throughout the Alabamian's senatorial discourse and debate were references to the classical and historical works he read. This practice so impressed his colleagues that they often addressed him as the "Scholarly Senator." The reiteration of these insights involved more than mere rhetorical flourish or an attempt to provide increased authority for a particular argument. He agreed with one of his favorite ancient authors, Thucydides, that individuals in the same situation would react similarly unless they had learned from history that a particular course of action would bring disaster. He also concurred with Polybius that without constitutional checks rulers would inevitably abuse their power, thereby creating a popular contempt for law that could end democracy. Finally, he assumed that the struggle between Thomas Jefferson and Alexander Hamilton during the nation's early years represented opposing values and policies paralleling Republicans' and Democrats' conflicting approaches to the Great Depression.

Guided by these assumptions, Black attacked Hoover's policies. When the President proposed that the Federal Farm Bureau use control of credit to limit agricultural production in order to increase prices, Black objected. "Mr. Jefferson in one of his letters stated," he told the Senate, "that when the time came that he could be directed from Washington when to sow and when to reap and how much to plant and how much to reap, the days of the independence of the farmer would be at an end." Moreover, Black condemned Hoover's rigid opposition to federally funded relief for the unemployed, while the President condoned funneling federal assistance to big business through the Reconstruction Finance Corporation.

The senator also criticized the highly protectionist Smoot-Hawley Tariff. He attempted, unsuccessfully, to amend the bill with a five-year prohibition on foreign immigration. Though this was purportedly an attempt to protect native American labor, critics argued that Black's plan reflected less solicitude for workers than a racist anti-immigrant position. At the same time, however, Black fought to protect the free circulation of ideas. Citing Jefferson's ideas as justification, he won revision of an amendment that conferred upon customs inspectors the authority to ban certain books from the United States.

Black also voted against Hoover's nominations for the Supreme Court. He unsuccessfully opposed the seating of Charles Evans Hughes as chief justice after the death of William Howard Taft in 1930. He was on the winning side shortly thereafter, however, when the Senate refused to confirm John J. Parker's appointment as associate justice.

Black believed in vigorous governmental regulation of big business and giant corporations, which he blamed for the economic collapse. Consequently, he fought Hoover's nomination of two former corporate lawyers to the Interstate Commerce Commission because they would, he was sure, support business rather than the public interest. Nevertheless, when Wisconsin progressive Republican Robert M. La Follette, Jr., and Colorado Democrat Edward P. Costigan proposed a Federal Emergency Relief Board, Black joined Hoover in opposing the creation of a national administrative agency empowered to disburse $375,000,000 to dispossessed Americans. Black objected to reliance on centralized federal authority. "How much more in line it is with the principles of Jefferson," he told the Senate, "not to say that the money shall be distributed in Alabama and Colorado" according to "rules established by a Washington bureau but to let them have the money directly, and then trust the States and the people to distribute it as they should." Black proposed a substitute measure providing for relief administered by the states. The *Nation* was quick to charge Black with a base motive for the shift: "Black of Alabama" became "Hysterical over the prospect of a federal relief plan which might feed Negroes as well as whites." A coalition of Republican administration regulars and southern Democrats, however, defeated both Black's proposal and the original La Follette-Costigan bill.

By contrast, Black enthusiastically endorsed federal development of Muscle Shoals. Norris had doggedly pushed for federal control of electric energy and nitrate production throughout the Tennessee River Valley. Hoover, campaigning for President in 1928, suggested that he would support the proposal, whereupon Norris reintroduced and won passage of his legislation. But Hoover vetoed it on grounds of economy. Black condemned what he regarded as the President's duplicity. Black charged that Hoover had sold out to the "power trust," which, the senator asserted, made enormous profits while unemployed Americans suffered.

The electric ultilities' victory reinforced Black's conviction that impersonal corporate and bureaucratic structures exploited economic chaos. In the name of efficiency, Black told the Senate, the Hoover administration's policies encouraged monopoly, depriving individuals of the independence upon which respectability depended. The specter of material dependency, however, was not the sole evil. As a nation of "a few business masters and many clerks and servants" emerged, democracy itself was at risk because the community lost the individual's contribution to local affairs as an independent thinker and executive. The claim that corporate consolidation was efficient made monopoly the order of the day, concentrating more and more power in the hands of the few.

As Black fought these battles Alabama was rarely out of his mind. He got Congress to pass private bills to assist individual constituents. When the Senate was not in session Black, Josephine, and the two boys returned to Birmingham. Black closely followed the Alabama political scene, relying on family friends to gain an accurate picture of conditions. The organization loyalists Black had joined during the 1928 presidential campaign refused to allow anyone who had then bolted the party to be a Democratic candidate in 1930. As a result, Tom Heflin, Alabama's senior senator, could not seek the Democratic nomination, and ran in the general election against the party's nominee, John H. Bankhead, Jr., who won all but ten of sixty-seven counties. The victory demonstrated that the Alabama Democratic establishment was again in full control. Although Black initially vacillated, in the name of party loyalty he finally endorsed Bankhead, the man he had defeated in 1926. Black exhorted Alabamians to defend the party of Jefferson, Wilson, and Robert E. Lee against that of Hamilton, Grant, and Hoover. "We cannot," he exclaimed, "we will not, we must not destroy the party which brought the sunlight of peace, happiness, and security to the white men and women of Alabama."

With Bankhead's triumph Black became his state's senior senator. He had aligned himself with the political powers he had once opposed. Charging ballot fraud, Heflin convinced the Senate to conduct an investigation of the election. Nevertheless, after the inquiry a majority voted to seat Bankhead. Black's stand for party loyalty during the dispute won ringing praise from Bankhead's brother, Will. "I hope that all of our friends," he wrote Democratic stalwarts, "will support Senator Black." This support was vital because Alabama Democrats had again changed the rules governing primary elections, making a run-off necessary if the first-place candidate did not receive a clear majority. Since the Klan and prohibitionists remained divided, the new rules benefited those who received the endorsement of the Democratic establishment.

These realities undoubtedly concerned Black, who was up for reelection in 1932. To build popular support he attacked Hoover and resisted, unavailingly, the proposal to establish the Reconstruction Finance Corporation. Fervently, though unsuccessfully, he defended the interests of small farmers and tenants against Hoover's policy of funding big landholders through the Federal Farm Board. Reflecting growing dissatisfaction with prohibition, Black sided with Norris in advocating modification of the Eighteenth Amendment. He and Norris were allied, too, in the continuing effort to establish federal ownership of Muscle Shoals. Moreover, white Alabamians' fear that blacks might receive equal benefits probably influenced their senator's vote against the La Follette-Costigan Relief Bill.

Indeed, prior to the 1932 election racial tensions were mounting. For years the Scottsboro case agitated Alabama, the South, and the nation. Convicted for rapes allegedly occurring on a north Alabama freight train, eight young blacks faced death sentences, or, in the case of one thirteen-year-old, life imprisonment. The flimsy evidence supporting the convictions and the hurried trials suggested a lack of elemental due process. Judicial proceedings and appeals ultimately lasted twenty years. To represent the eight youths the NAACP hired white Birmingham lawyers, while at the same time attempting to cooperate with the International Labor Defense, the legal arm of the Communist party. Cooperation collapsed, however, and the ILD alone conducted the defense. In Alabama during 1931 and 1932 the combination of racial conflict and communist involvement set off confrontations in which whites and blacks died. A citizen's letter to the governor reflected the view of whites: so long as the Scottsboro "negro rapists" remained alive, the "reds" would use their cause to "incite our colored people to riot, rape, and kill." Black's close friend and former law partner, William E. Fort, was one of the lawyers the NAACP hired. Although the media and his former associate kept him informed, Black remained aloof, instead emphasizing economic affairs.

The 1932 election was for both Alabama's senior senator and the president of the United States. In the state primary Black faced an old opponent, former governor Thomas E. Kilby, who climaxed his campaign by publicizing a photostatic copy of the "Grand Passport" Black had received from the Klan years before. Under the new primary rules the race resulted in a runoff. Undaunted, Black used radio broadcasts to popularize his fight for economic welfare and respectability, and with the combined support of the Democratic establishment and labor, Black carried 52 of 67 counties to win the runoff. Confident of victory in the state's general election, Black campaigned for Roosevelt throughout the nation. "I am subject to your call from now until the last vote is counted," he wrote FDR, who replied, "Keep in touch." Although party loyalty and hope for advancement may have drawn Black to Roosevelt, increasingly a strong personal bond developed until Black regularly described Roosevelt as "magnificent." Both won handily in the fall, and Americans looked forward to the New Deal.

Neither Roosevelt nor such faithful followers as Black knew exactly what the New Deal meant. It was not surprising that Americans should overwhelmingly approve greater federal control of the economy and social welfare. Nevertheless, between 1933 and 1935 considerable disagreement existed among New Dealers. Black and Harvard Law professor Felix Frankfurter were among those urging stringent regulation of big corporations and strict enforcement of antitrust laws. They favored regulation through agencies such as the Interstate Commerce Commission but distrusted enlarged federal control in the name of centralized planning. Another group defended the need for planning by bureaucratic experts whose skill enabled them to understand and remedy social and economic problems. Hoover would have done better to increase the scale of centralized government management until it matched that of big business. The failure of Hoover's voluntary cooperation demonstrated that the federal government should possess sufficient coercive authority to protect and encourage stable business and social welfare. Neither the planners nor the antitrust regulators wanted big government to destroy capitalism; rather, they wanted government to save capitalism from itself.

These tensions shaped Roosevelt's initial New Deal programs. From 1933 to 1935 Black and his colleagues in the Democrat-controlled Congress passed numerous laws that delegated unprecedented peacetime power to the President and an enlarged federal bureaucracy. The Federal Emergency Relief Administration (FERA) and other federal agencies funneled millions of dollars through state governments into local communities to provide individuals and families with food, clothing, and shelter. Federally funded public works also provided jobs for millions of Americans. The Agricultural Adjustment Administration (AAA) took primary responsibility for the management of the nation's agriculture, while banking and credit came under stricter federal regulation. The New Deal also repealed prohibition and took part in electrical power production and distribution by enacting the Tennessee Valley Authority (TVA).

These measures reflected compromises between the planners and the antitrust regulators. In each case Black supported accommodation. Such divergent influences left the impact of the New Deal ambiguous. Federal relief and public works projects sustained the self-respect of individuals and the welfare of communities. From a spiritual standpoint they yielded a rich harvest in increased hope, self-reliance, and confidence. The AAA, however, was different. Concerned principally with economic efficiencies arising from large agricultural units, its bureaucrats and experts focused their attention on big planters. As a result land owners in Mississippi, Arkansas, and Texas received \$2.5 million, \$2.1 million, and \$1.2 million, respectively, whereas those in Louisiana and Alabama were allotted only \$413,000 and \$130,000. Moreover, a disproportionate amount of AAA funding—\$7 million worth—went to big landlords and corporations rather than to small farmers and tenants. Although Black had opposed Hoover's federal agricultural program, he willingly accommodated federal intervention imposed by Democrats.

The New Deal did little to improve the lot of blacks. Although some occupied lower- and middle-level positions in many New Deal programs, they rarely escaped regulations enforcing racial segregation; and the AAA ignored black tenants and small farmers or even forced them off the land. The TVA record, Senator Black knew all too well, was also mixed. Blacks excluded from jobs during initial construction eventually were employed on a rigidly segregated basis.

The relief and public works programs, however, benefited blacks somewhat. The legislation establishing the FERA categorically banned racial discrimination. Although southern representatives weakened the enforcement of this provision, the relief measures nonetheless helped the blacks to survive during the worst Depression years. The Public Works Administration, headed by former Chicago NAACP president Harold Ickes, moreover, went further than others in fighting racial discrimination. Despite repeated attacks from Southerners, Ickes faithfully implemented the policy "that Congress intended this program to be carried out without discrimination." Senator Black, for his part, supported the equal rights of whites and blacks under the New Deal relief policies, though he did not resist racial segregation in their administration. Aware, moreover, that employers would prefer whites over blacks if wages were nationally uniform, he countenanced a lower rate for blacks to ensure their access to public jobs.

In confrontations with ocean shippers and airlines, Black discovered the benefits and risks of enlarged federal authority. After the 1932 Democratic victory he became chairman of a special subcommittee investigating mail contracts between the federal government and representatives of these two transportation industries. With Roosevelt's blessing Black pushed the committee's power to the limit. At one point he sent the Senate's sergeant-at-arms, sporting a silver cane, long black coat, dark striped trousers, a ten-gallon cowboy hat, and a red carnation, to arrest a former Republican official who had avoided appearing. On another occasion investigators roused a New Jersey man at one o'clock in the morning and rushed him to testify in Washington. In addition, the committee dramatically enlarged its power to subpoena evidence, resulting in court cases charging violation of the Fourth Amendment. It also tried, convicted, and sentenced to ten-day jail terms uncooperative witnesses. Although the courts upheld such actions, critics condemned them as "worthy of Fascism, Hitlerism, or Sovietism at their best." Black's investigation revealed that shipping and airline officials had engaged in extensive misconduct. As a result, Congress established the Federal Aviation Commission to regulate the entire airline industry and tightened federal administrative control of shipping.

On New Deal policy governing industrial and labor relations, Black struck an advanced position. As soon as Roosevelt took office in March, 1933, Black proposed prohibiting the sale or distribution in interstate commerce of manufacturing and mining goods produced by workers laboring more than 6 hours a day or 30 hours a week, the purpose being to foster employment by sharing the work. Unlike New Dealers who favored stimulating industrial production through centralized planning, Black hoped to increase demand while avoiding enlarged government, though in point of fact the proposal was an unrealistic remedy like many others of the time.

Although the Thirty-hour Week Bill passed the Senate, Roosevelt stalled it in the House. Black wrote a Birmingham constituent that "my 30 hour bill has been stopped" because the "President has indicated that he is going to send a message asking for some kind of substitute." In May, 1933, Roosevelt introduced the National Industrial Recovery Act (NIRA). Despite opposition from Black and others during the debate over the proposal, Congress enacted the law, creating the National Recovery Administration, empowered to oversee the formulation of codes governing prices, labor, and production in manufacturing and mining industries, thus virtually suspending the antitrust laws to foster cooperation, expand production, raise prices, and improve profitability. Despite significant reservations Black, the Roosevelt loyalist, ultimately voted for the NIRA.

Meanwhile, he never lost faith in a policy emphasizing employment and demand rather than centralized planning and bureaucratic control. Black absolutely believed in increased democracy as a remedy for society's ills. Government encouraged democracy when it curbed powerful interests through regulation and antitrust laws. Government threatened democracy, however, if it substituted the will of unelected planners and experts for that of the people and their representatives. The Thirty-hour Week Bill imposed restrictions on industry rather than relying on centralized administration. Preserving popular control over industrial relations encouraged respectability and the interdependency of individual and community welfare. By increasing employment Black hoped to give workers a stake in the community and also to foster their involvement in self-government.

By 1935 Black's misgivings were secondary, however, for Roosevelt's New Deal was in deep trouble. Early in that year the Supreme Court unanimously struck down the NIRA as unconstitutional. In *Schechter Poultry Corporation* v. *U.S.*, the Court held that Congress had delegated such unprecedented peacetime power to the President to manage industrial relations that it constituted "delegation run riot." Black reintroduced the Thirty-hour Week Bill, but again it was defeated. Moreover, within a year the Court declared much of the New Deal legislation, including the AAA, unconstitutional. The judiciary's actions came particularly close to home when federal Judge Grubb, Black's former courtroom adversary and longtime political supporter, held that TVA's sale of electricity to Alabama Power was unlawful. The Supreme Court ultimately decided in favor of TVA, small conciliation given the fate of the rest of the New Deal.

Defeat in the Supreme Court was not the only blow to Roosevelt's policies. On the extreme right and left a fascist movement and the Communist party were vocal advocates of increased authoritarianism and radicalism. By contrast, the 1928 Democratic presidential candidate, Al Smith, and the former chairman of the Democratic National Committee, John J. Raskob, aligned with Republicans, charged that the New Deal was too extreme. The most popular opponents were dissidents who had initially supported Roosevelt: Dr. Francis E. Townsend, Father Charles E. Coughlin, and Louisiana's Senator

Huey P. Long. Townsend especially received growing attention for his proposal that the federal government pay employed Americans aged sixty years and older a pension if they retired, thus opening up jobs for the unemployed. However, none received greater attention than Long, who vigorously pushed a "Share-Our-Wealth Plan," according to which the federal government would tax the rich and use the proceeds to guarantee each American family a minimum homestead and a yearly wage of $2,500. Moreover, faithful New Dealers such as Senator Robert F. Wagner of New York called for a national agency to defend the rights of organized labor and enlarge the federal power to punish lynchings. In addition, many New Dealers demanded that agriculture receive further federal assistance.

As the election year of 1936 approached, Roosevelt skillfully mobilized Democrats and national public opinion. With the help of Black and other loyalists, the Roosevelt administration introduced legislation that became the Social Security Act, providing elderly workers a monthly income. Although the measure exempted domestics and agricultural laborers, which included many blacks, it did establish federal unemployment insurance, aid to dependent mothers and children, and assistance to the blind and crippled. Congress passed the administration's expanded Agricultural Adjustment Act. Despite his personal disapproval, Roosevelt signed into law the Wagner Act, creating the National Labor Relations Board, which protected the rights of labor unions. Roosevelt also won passage of the Public Utility Holding Company Act and other legislation imposing new federal restrictions on corporate organization and consolidation. A "soak the rich" tax on corporations and the nation's wealthiest citizens also became law. Congress also passed an enlarged public works program and federally funded farm and urban mortgage assistance, programs that used the principle of cooperation between federal and state governments and that won the support of neo-Jeffersonians such as Black.

Black's support was important to Roosevelt's campaign. Attacking the "wildly extravagant proposals" and "impossible schemes" of Long and Townsend, Black defended the Administration's Social Security Bill before such groups as New York City's American Association for Social Security. He helped to gain equal Social Security benefits for blacks as well as whites. His dogged campaign for the Thirty-hour Week Bill laid the groundwork, too, for renewed debate over the Fair Labor Standards bill, establishing a minimum wage and maximum hours and abolishing child labor. He was also with the majority when Congress voted to make the wage paid to employees on public works projects equal to the rate prevailing locally in the private sector. Black vigorously defended the revitalized Agricultural Adjustment Act and higher tax rates on corporate profits.

Always a fervent defender of labor, Black actively supported the Wagner Act. Since 1933 the United Mine Workers in Birmingham had struggled to reverse the defeats of 1908 and 1920. Nevertheless, racial tensions aroused conflicts between skilled white workers represented by the American Federation of Labor and the mass of black industrial laborers. When the Steel Workers Organizing Committee sought to establish a biracial union structure, a white steel worker exclaimed: "I'm not going to join your damn nigger organization." Nevertheless, federal intervention under the NIRA had facilitated real interracial cooperation. As one union leader noted, he was "not seeking to elevate the negro, but experience teaches us that if the negro is not unionized" by the "side of the white worker, he will be used as a strike breaker to kill the union movement." Black saw in the NLRB's control of labor-management relations great benefits for all workers, regardless of race.

Black received most national publicity for his role in passage of the Public Utility Holding Company Act. As the Congress debated a controversial provision requiring the breakup or "death sentence" of certain giant corporations, many Democrats and Republicans attacked it as extreme. Senators and congressmen began receiving an unprecedented number of telegrams and letters, purportedly from constituents, condemning the measure. Roosevelt urged Black, who chaired a committee responsible for drafting legislation controlling lobbyists, to investigate. Black and Indiana Senator Sherman Minton employed the same controversial tactics used during the airline and shipping inquiries; newspapers condemned them as "Nazi methods." The American Civil Liberties Union warned that the committee was establishing a dangerous precedent that could encourage harassment of progressive groups, minorities, and marginal political parties. Administration supporters also condemned Black for invading "the privacy which his liberal friends held more sacred than the legislation he was trying to help."

The investigators revealed, however, that corporate interests had organized and paid for the telegrams and letters attacking Roosevelt's bill. They also uncovered related questionable conduct on the part of other powerful business leaders. Ultimately, Congress passed a weaker version of the Holding Company Act with a modified "death sentence" clause, yet Black's efforts aroused popular support for both the New Deal and one of its most loyal defenders. Finally Black answered his critics in a *Harper's* article: "Special privilege thrives in secrecy and darkness, and is destroyed by the rays of pitiless publicity."

Black and Roosevelt himself took their most problematic stand on Wagner's Antilynch Bill. After World War I and the ascendancy of the Ku Klux Klan, statistics gathered by Alabama's Tuskegee Institute revealed a dramatic rise in lynching, which the Scottsboro case further exacerbated. As a result, Senators Wagner and Costigan, representing the NAACP, organized labor, and various humanitarian groups, introduced a bill enlarging the jurisdiction of federal courts in cases involving mobs. Black joined southern Democrats in filibustering the measure, thus holding up passage of the Social Security Act, the legislation establishing the NLRB, and other major New Deal legislation. Although Roosevelt personally favored the bill, he failed to press for it for reasons of political necessity. "The Southerners by reason of the seniority rule in Congress are chairmen or occupy strategic places on most of the Senate and House committees," the President explained. "If I come out for the anti-lynching bill now, they will block every bill I ask Congress to pass to keep America from collapsing. I just can't take that risk."

Black strongly opposed the Wagner-Costigan bill. He condemned lynching as an evil, but equated increased federal judicial power with the Yankee intervention during Reconstruction. History demonstrated, he said, that Reconstruction had failed because it aroused southern public opinion against what had been growing sympathy for racial justice. Unwise enforcement of the Fourteenth Amendment, jeopardizing local control of the criminal justice system, had particularly angered white Southerners. As a result, the advocates of voting rights and education for "those who had only recently been slaves" were defeated once "others" entered the states "on account of laws that were enacted at this Capitol [Washington, D.C.] for political advantage. Had that not been done," Black claimed, "the solution of the great problem of two races living together side by side would not have been so much retarded." The South's experience paralleled that of Norman England as described by Macaulay, in that frequently laws "designed for the most benign purposes fail" because lawmakers forget that "unless we desire to turn over the administration of the laws to the military authorities, in the final analysis we must depend upon the sentiments of those who enter the jury box."

Black went further still. Labor was mistaken in supporting the antilynching measure because the Supreme Court had interpreted the Fourteenth Amendment to grant corporations the rights of natural persons. Corporations could therefore use the law against strikers on the ground that the threat to private property was tantamount to a lynch mob's violation of individual rights. Behind such efforts, Black warned, were the "same predatory and privileged interests that practically brought us to destruction at the end of 1929." Wagner and other New Dealers, he believed, had unknowingly aligned themselves with the "apostles of special privilege and greed." This in turn impeded passage of the Social Security Act, which would "affect millions and millions of American men and women, irrespective of race or creed or color." Citing Jefferson's long-standing opposition to federal courts, Black also expressed his preference for the "justice of the people" enforced by juries and elected state courts rather than that of "judges appointed for life." Though he favored increased federal regulatory economic authority exceeding that intended by the Framers of the Constitution, it was necessary, he said, because the nation faced "a new condition and a new economic era." At the same time, the federal government should accept distinctions in "habits and customs" among the states.

The battle over the Antilynch Bill suggested the limits of the New Deal. Wagner, Norris, and Black took the lead in enlarging federal power to manage the corporate and agricultural economy, preserve the interests of workers and consumers, improve the material conditions of communities, and foster individual respectability. The defeat of Wagner's Antilynch Bill revealed, however, the extent to which New Dealers were divided. Black and Roosevelt, in subordinating protection of individual rights to narrower political necessities, argued that federal intervention on behalf of racial justice jeopardized national efforts to improve the economic opportunity of all Americans regardless of race. Black's appeals to Jeffersonian democracy and human nature in opposing the Antilynch Bill, however, obscured neither his own shortsightedness nor a vital question: should government uplift the community's welfare without safeguarding the rights of individuals?

The answer seemed clear as Roosevelt ran for reelection during 1936. Black's fervent support for the New Deal brought him into the inner circle of Roosevelt's campaign advisers. He stumped throughout the nation against the Republican candidate Alfred M. Landon. At one point Landon responded by condemning Black's congressional investigatory tactics as having "openly and flagrantly violated the constitutional restrictions against unreasonable search and seizure." Above all, however, the Republicans argued that the New Deal's reliance on big government amounted to a cure for the Depression worse than the disease. Black responded that "national business control, as distinguished from local business control, has made it necessary that many of us reshape and maybe remold traditional concepts that we really love." Most Southerners, indeed most Americans, agreed with this reasoning. By contrast, since the Scottsboro case continued to arouse racial violence and fears of "commie" radicalism, Southerners were equally adamant that federal authority should not extend to race relations.

Even so, the Republican attempt to make the election a referendum against the New Deal utterly failed. Except for Maine and Vermont, Roosevelt carried every state, receiving the largest popular vote in history to that time. In the wake of the victory the Democrat-controlled Congress introduced new programs extending still further the federal government's influence in American life. Although Black again introduced his Thirty-hour Week Bill, he gradually gave it up in favor of a revised Fair Labor Standards Act. Intense opposition developed from southern Democrats who condemned the provisions for a nationally uniform minimum wage and regulated hours as well as the end of child labor. Nevertheless, quoting Dickens and Macaulay on factory reforms in nineteenth-century England, Black modified his earlier resistance to equal wages for whites and blacks. "I subscribe to the gospel that a man who is born in Alabama and who can do as much work as a man born in any state in New England, is," he said, "entitled to the same pay if he does the same work." When a Mississippi senator scorned some of the impressionistic language Black had incorporated in the bill as "a lot of lovely poetry," Black exclaimed: "All through the ages, poets have raised their voices in behalf of the weak." This sort of congressional leadership, combined with his prominent role in the President's reelection victory, led some newspaper commentators and a few labor leaders to discuss Black seriously as a possible successor to Roosevelt in 1940.

Ironically, despite Roosevelt's impressive triumph, a fundamental question existed as to whether the programs enacted after the *Schechter* decision could survive review by the Supreme Court. As a result, Roosevelt introduced legislation giving the President power to nominate to the Court an additional justice for each one over age seventy who chose not to retire on a liberal pension. He would thus receive the opportunity to name up to six new appointees. Although he justified the measure on the ground of improved efficiency, it clearly attempted to stack the Court with New Deal supporters.

As soon as the "court-packing plan" reached the Senate early in 1937, opposition erupted nationally. As the bill was read in the Senate, Vice President John Nance Garner held his nose and then turned thumbs down. Because the plan undercut the Constitution's separation of powers and checks and balances, even some liberals opposed it. Privately, southern Democrats also feared that a Court packed with Roosevelt's appointees might sustain laws such as the Fair Labors Standards Act, which in turn might eventually erode racial segregation.

One of the few Southerners who defended the court-packing plan during the winter, spring, and summer of 1937 was Hugo Black. On nationwide radio he asserted that a "majority of our judges should not amend the Constitution according to their economic predilections every time they decide a case." At the same time, however, he certainly agreed that the President had the power to appoint New Dealers as justices. He equated Roosevelt with President Taft, who had suggested that he wanted judges who would "construe the [Fourteenth Amendment's] due process clause" according to the prevailing sentiment of the country. Black thus criticized judges who read the Constitution in light of their own economic attitudes, while praising those whose views were consistent with the nation's "prevailing sentiment." Jefferson and Andrew Jackson had based their choice of justices on whether the nominee accepted the dominant political party's policies, and Black uged FDR to do the same. Such arguments proved inadequate against the bipartisan coalition, however, and, after Roosevelt's principal legislative leader, Arkansas Senator Joe Robinson died in July, 1937, the President's proposal died as well.

The defeat of the court-packing plan revealed a growing split among Democrats. On one side were those such as Wagner and Black who wanted to remedy the social and economic injustices they believed had accumulated since the decline of progressivism. At odds with them were many southern Democrats who believed that such measures as the NLRB and the Fair

Labor Standards Bill went too far, particularly because they threatened racial segregation. Increasingly, the media and Roosevelt himself explained the division as a split between liberals and conservatives. As early as 1928 Hoover had described his program as "true liberalism," attacking "free-for-all and devil-take-the-hindmost. The very essence of equality of opportunity and of American individualism" was that it demanded "economic justice as well as political and social justice." For Hoover the proper role of the federal government in protecting liberalism was merely that of an "umpire instead of a player in the economic game." Once this approach failed during the Depression, New Dealers began equating liberalism with increased federal control. Not until after the Court fight revealed growing resistance to still greater federal authority, however, did administration loyalists more generally identify themselves as New Deal liberals opposed by the "conservative coalition."

Black's identification with the liberal wing of the Democratic party produced unexpected benefits. In May 1937, Justice Willis Van Devanter, one of the Court's staunchest opponents of the New Deal, notified Roosevelt of his retirement. Not until the President knew that the court-packing plan was lost did he nominate a candidate. Seeking the advice only of his attorney general and one or two others, he narrowed the choice to two senators, Minton and Black. For some time Josephine had urged her husband to return to law practice, particularly as the two young boys had begun attending an expensive military academy in Florida. Sterling's hearing problem also required costly regular medical treatment. Moreover, they now had a third child, Josephine, born five years earlier. Although few doubted that Black could win reelection in 1938, he was nonetheless worried. Alabama newspapers had attacked his defense of the Court plan and the Fair Labor Standards Bill, and his defense of strikers in north Alabama exacerbated such criticism.

Finally, however, Black accepted Roosevelt's nomination, and on August 12 the Senate was so notified. Roosevelt had proceeded with such confidentiality that initially the Senate reacted to Vice President Garner's reading of the message which began "I nominate Hugo L. Black" with stunned silence. Then, just as quickly, the call arose to delay voting, and for the first time since the 1880s a President's appointment of a sitting senator went to a committee for investigation.

According to the *New York Times,* the nomination "dropped like salt into political wounds already rubbed raw by the court issue." Other long-standing reasons involved Black's whole Senate career. To most Senate colleagues he remained a loner, presenting, the *Times* observed, two personalities: the "cool and philosophical student of motive" and the "crusading harrier of men." Even liberals had questioned his tactics during the subcommittee investigations. Another critic drove the point home: Black possessed the ability to be one of the nation's foremost senators "were it not for the fact that he still thinks in terms of the time when he was prosecuting attorney."

Despite a near fistfight at one point during the debate, the subcommittee and then the committee voted for Black's confirmation, 5–1 and 13–4. As the issue moved to the full Senate, however, the NAACP and the Socialist party sent telegrams to senators urging that he be questioned about his silence on the Scottsboro case, opposition to the Antilynch Bill, and, above all, reputed membership in the Ku Klux Klan. Rumors of Klan affiliation reached the White House, whereupon the ailing Norris defended Black. "He is a worthy representative of the common people," Norris said publicly. "He understands their hopes and ambitions, and their liberties in his hands will be safe." Questions concerning the Klan, however, continued. Reporters contacted the Imperial Wizard Hiram Evans in Atlanta, who answered that as far as he knew Black was neither a member nor a sympathizer. Of course, they did not know that Black and Evans had been boyhood friends in Clay County and fellow Klansmen in Birmingham. Except to urge anyone concerned about the Klan-membership issue to vote against confirmation, Black remained silent. He knew the truth, but refrained from jeopardizing his appointment by admitting it.

Finally, despite mounting public clamor and criticism on the Senate floor from Republicans and southern Democrats, the administration won Black's confirmation by a vote of 63–16.

Although southern senators attacked Black, they did not vote against him. According to Ickes, they "'God-damned' the nomination all over the place when it was first announced [but] didn't have the courage to stand up and vote against a fellow senator from the Deep South."

Ickes alone was present when Roosevelt presented Black his commission. The Alabamian, Ickes wrote in his diary, "made no attempt to disguise the very genuine pleasure that his appointment gave him. He was delighted." Public response was mixed. "My cup runneth over," Senator Minton told the President, and Frankfurter also expressed enthusiasm. *BusinessWeek* was more analytical: "Black will no longer have to demagogue to keep his head above water. No longer can the 'princes of privilege' down in Alabama threaten his political existence." A writer for *Newsweek* was even less charitable, observing that there "have been worse appointments to high judicial office," but "I can't remember where or when." Hoover was still more to the point, noting that the Court was "one-ninth packed."

Traditionally, new justices waited until the Court's term began to take the requisite oaths of office. Without explanation, however, Black arranged to have them administered shortly after receiving the commission. Very likely, to avoid risking his position further because of the Klan controversy, he sought the early swearing in to make the appointment irreversible. On August 19 he became an associate justice of the United States Supreme Court, serving "during good behavior" for life. He and Josephine then embarked for a trip to Europe before the Court's work began in October.

But the Klan controversy did not die. Two reporters went south to explore what connection if any had or still existed between Black and the Invisible Empire. Soon, nationwide headlines reported Black's earlier Klan affiliation, and polls showed that public opinion was split 60/40 against his serving as a Supreme Court justice. Roosevelt fended off criticism of the appointment, confessing that he had never thought to inquire about Black's past and suggesting that some sort of public explanation was in order. At the same time, however, little attention was given to the statement of Alabama's governor that years before he and Black had "belonged to the Klan" just as they had "belonged to every other Protestant organization." Similarly, a leader of Birmingham's Jewish community was ignored when he said, "Mr. Black is as much of a friend to Jews and Catholics as anybody."

Although reporters pursued Black in Europe he refused to comment until he returned to the United States. When the National Broadcasting Corporation offered him national radio time to discuss the issue, he accepted. On October 1, at the suburban Washington home of close personal friends, with newsmen waiting outside, a few family members and friends joined an estimated 30 million Americans to hear Black's remarks.

Traditionally, Supreme Court justices did not publicly comment on controversial issues, he said, but this was an "extraordinary occasion." Americans, he contended, were the object of a "concerted campaign" seeking to foment religious prejudices in order to convince them that Black was the enemy of minorities. Arguing that his Senate record refuted such charges, he affirmed an absolute commitment to the religious protections of the Bill of Rights. "I did join the Klan, I never rejoined. What appeared then or what appears now on the records of that organization, I do not know," he asserted. As for the "unsolicited card" he had received, he had not looked upon it as "a membership of any kind" in the Klan. "I never used it. I did not even keep it." Upon becoming a senator he never again had any involvement with the organization, Justice Black claimed, and he assured the audience that he counted many Catholics, Jews, and Negroes among his close friends. Finally, he declared, "my discussion of this question is closed."

Response to Black's address was divided. Supporters applauded his candor. Opponents described the speech as merely an effort at "trimming his political sails to fit the prevailing wind." A few racial and religious minority groups were outraged. As one spokesman said, "Negroes will be satisfied with nothing less than prompt and effective action designed to remove this blot from the escutcheon of the judiciary." Roosevelt, however, told a close adviser that the speech "was a grand job. It did the trick. You just wait and see." Indeed, a late October poll showed that American public opinion now favored Black's serving as a justice by 56 to 44 percent.

On one level the episode displayed little more than expediency, consistent with Black's silence during the Senate investigation and his early swearing in as a justice. Yet the struggle over Black's elevation to the Supreme Court also suggested deeper strains within New Deal liberalism. The President nominated the Alabamian primarily because of his consistent, effective support for expanded federal power to remedy the nation's social and economic ills. New Dealers themselves, however, were divided concerning both the scope and nature of bigger federal government: antitrust regulators resisted bureaucratic planning, while southern defenders of segregation adamantly opposed federal protection of civil rights. But despite the rejection of the Fair Labor Standard Bill, most southern Democrats overwhelmingly voted with liberals to maintain increased federal responsibility for agriculture, the TVA, Social Security, and other welfare programs. Similarly, liberals such as Black and Wagner agreed on extensive federal intervention in favor of workers, but were on opposite sides when it came to civil rights.

Fundamentally, these conflicts represented an intractable dilemma regarding the extent to which big government's costs offset its benefits. Black took his seat on the Court during October 1937. With the values learned, tested, and refined since Clay County, he confronted the dilemma of American liberalism.

CHAPTER FIVE

Liberal Justice (1937–1941)

❖
❖

For Black the Supreme Court was a new forum in which to fight for New Deal liberalism. The Brethren were embroiled in continuing conflicts exacerbated by the interplay between the individual assumptions of the justices and the need to win a majority vote in each case. Though Roosevelt's New Deal and his liberal Court clearly were secure by 1941, the struggle over liberalism did not end.

Washington, D.C., became the family's permanent residence. Hugo and Josephine purchased a house built near the end of the eighteenth century in Alexandria, Virginia. Located in a compact neighborhood at the beginning of a slope running down to the Potomac River, the new home afforded considerable privacy. A garden and tennis court provided members of the family diversion in a life relatively uncomplicated by the capital's social calendar and political pressures.

This life was never insulated from the intimate joys and demands of parenthood. Hugo, Jr., and Sterling were attending a military academy in Florida, while daughter Josephine remained in a Washington school. Hugo had respiratory problems and Sterling a hearing deficiency, but their devoted parents did all they could to ensure that the boys had a normal educational experience. Early in 1938 the justice wrote the school's superintendent, pleased "that the boys are making such good records" but also expressing concern about some new condition Hugo had developed. In addition, he noted that

"Sterling's defective hearing has given him a great deal of trouble," making his "work more difficult." Because of the physical separation during the school year, the family maintained a regular correspondence. Both Black and Josephine were uneasy if a week went by without a letter.

This private life also included the justice's law clerks. These bright, young, recent law school graduates assisted in the research and writing of judicial opinions. Black's first clerk, Jerome Cooper, an Alabamian and Harvard Law School graduate, served for two years. Working closely with the Justice daily during each Court term, Cooper and his successors witnessed firsthand the development of Black's constitutional thinking. Although they discussed opinions in the justice's Supreme Court chambers, their exchanges often occurred in the upstairs corner study of the Black home, continuing hours into the night. In this study Black not only wrote his opinions but continued his self-education, adding steadily to his already extensive private library. Participating intimately in this intellectual process, the clerks learned of the integral relationship between Black's books and his constitutional ideas.

No clerk was long in the justice's service before Black urged him to read some volume of the classics or history. He always asked: "Have you read these books?" Usually the clerk answered in the negative, whereupon Black replied: "Well, they're your first assignment. What they have to say about human nature and history is more relevant than any thing I can think of to the issues now before the Court." Gradually the young lawyers perceived that the justice held that human nature was changeless. "Well, of course this has been the problem since the time of Tacitus," he would observe regarding some current issue. If the clerk said he had not read Tacitus, Black would retort, "Well, you can't be a lawyer if you haven't."

Black approached the members of the Court cordially and with respect. Not long after joining he wrote Justice Louis Brandeis concerning one of his opinions: "It is with real regret that I find myself unable to agree." Nevertheless, among men of equally strong egos and convictions Black's certainty of principle and confidence of understanding could seem offensive.

Brandeis privately remarked that Black had not "the faintest notion of what tolerance means, and while he talks a lot about democracy, he is totally devoid of its underlying demand which is tolerance in his own behavior." Undoubtedly the most extreme example, however, was Justice James R. McReynolds, who so detested Jews in general and Brandeis in particular that at one time he actually left the conference room whenever Brandeis spoke. These two justices apparently were never on speaking terms.

Black had joined a Court already fundamentally divided. Justices George Sutherland, Pierce Butler, and McReynolds adamantly stood against the New Deal's expansion of federal authority. Brandeis, Harlan F. Stone, and Benjamin Cardozo were generally supportive of Roosevelt's liberalism. Prior to the President's 1936 landslide victory, Chief Justice Charles Evans Hughes and Justice Owen Roberts generally had voted with those opposing the New Deal. After the election, however, Hughes convinced Roberts that further resistance was futile. The Chief Justice feared for the Court's independence if it continued to diverge radically from the needs and expectations of the American people. Early in 1937 the two joined the three liberals to sustain the constitutionality of the Wagner Act's National Labor Relations Board.

Many believed that this shift was the result of Roosevelt's court-packing plan. But, prior to the announcement of the plan, Hughes and Roberts had already decided privately to change their stance in a case involving the constitutionality of a Washington state minimum wage law. Shortly after the public expressed overwhelming support for Roosevelt in 1936, Roberts wrote a 5–4 majority opinion in *West Coast Hotel* v. *Parrish*, upholding the state law. Black's arrival on the Court in October 1937 seemed, then, to guarantee the liberals a clear majority.

With the same tenacity and creativity displayed since his youth, Black tackled his new judicial role. In order to familiarize himself with the evolution of the Court's constitutional doctrines, he examined systematically the more than three hundred volumes of reported decisions. Black was already a master of the procedural technicalities required in jury trials and appellate litigation. As a senator, he had displayed a grasp of the legislative process, including the constitutional principles governing the relations among the three branches of the federal government and between the federal and state governments. But the Supreme Court's function in the constitutional system was, he knew, unique. The Constitution rested on the principle that limitations were necessary to curb the excesses of majority rule. As a result in no democratic nation except the United States did unelected judges have such wide-ranging power to declare void the laws enacted by the people's representatives. In addition, the Court's nine justices were accountable only through the cumbersome process of impeachment, which had been used but once, and that time unsuccessfully.

As a lawyer and elected official Black had developed an independent philosophical basis for his actions, and he did the same as a justice. During the court-packing fight he had condemned judges for writing their economic views into judicial opinions. At the same time he had argued that courts should disregard precedents in order to uphold laws embodying economic principles conforming to the nation's changing needs and conditions. Black contended that judicial review, especially in the interpretation of the commerce clause, should take into account the "prevailing sentiments" of the people, at least insofar as these extended to technological innovation or economic change. Black did not deny the relevance of the Framers' purpose; they had intended, he believed, to establish a federal commerce power comprehending the needs of the entire nation.

Black's view grew out of a tension between rival constitutional theories of judicial activism and self-restraint. Throughout the early twentieth century Frankfurter and other critics attacked the Court's broad use of such constitutional provisions as the due process clauses of the Fourteenth and Fifth Amendments to strike down valuable social legislation. To counter what they regarded as unwarranted activism, the critics wanted judges to defer to lawmakers. Frankfurter did not deny that judicial review itself was vital in particular cases as a check on the excesses of majority rule. He rejected its wide-ranging use to protect property rights, however, urging judges instead to uphold the will of elected majorities.

As Black studied the decisions following the Court's dramatic shift of 1936–37, he found that to a considerable extent judicial activism had given way to self-restraint. In *NLRB* v. *Jones and Laughlin Steel Corp.* (1937), Hughes and Roberts joined Brandeis, Cardozo, and Stone, holding that under the Constitution's commerce clause Congress had the authority to establish the National Labor Relations Board. Less than two years earlier the Court had overturned similar uses of the commerce power. The new majority now rejected such precedents. deferring to the power of Congress to create a federal agency that would regulate labor relations as a component of interstate commerce. Shortly thereafter the Court applied the same restraint in sustaining the Social Security Act.

As Black examined other cases, however, he discovered that the Court had begun tentatively to pursue a more activist approach in another area. Throughout most of the nation's history the Court had affirmed that the Bill of Rights protected Americans from the federal government but not from state governments, but recently the justices had declared that certain "fundamental" guarantees in the Bill of Rights applied also to litigants in state courts. Black himself would become a champion of the doctrine that the freedoms guaranteed in the First Amendment applied to the states through the due process clause of the Fourteenth Amendment.

From the beginning, Justice Black displayed independence in attempting to reconcile the tension between activism and restraint. During his first three years, the Court decided twenty-six cases involving the power of administrative agencies, particularly the NLRB. The Court reversed the agency's decisions only five times, and in each of these cases Black dissented because he felt the majority had not adhered closely enough to Congress's purpose in establishing the agencies.

The justice was closer to fellow liberals in other commerce clause cases. From 1937 on, none of them fundamentally disagreed with his view that congressional power to regulate business activity was coextensive with the national economic order. He also voted with Stone and the majority upholding state power to regulate the length and width of vehicles using highways. Black's view on the power to tax businesses involved in interstate trade was not accepted, however, when the liberal majority refused to sanction certain state taxes because they discriminated against others.

On matters traditionally considered within the judiciary's purview, Black was also relatively independent. Since the decision of *Swift* v. *Tyson* (1842) federal judges had claimed an independent authority to determine for themselves what law should apply in suits involving the status of state court decisions in federal tribunals. But in *Erie Railroad* v. *Tompkins* (1938) Brandeis declared that such discretion unconstitutionally interfered with the deference owed to state courts. Joining the majority, Black wrote Brandeis privately that the decision was one of his "best" and that was "saying much." Even so, Black also informed Brandeis that he had written a dissent in an earlier case urging the same result as that achieved in *Erie.*

This willingness to challenge even established doctrines governing judicial powers extended still further. For decades American courts had held that corporations were persons enjoying the protections of the Fourteenth Amendment. Black had opposed this principle because it enabled corporate defendants to avoid state regulations and courts. Thus, dissenting in *Connecticut General Life* v. *Johnson* (1938), Black urged a wholesale reevaluation of hundreds of precedents on the ground that they violated the original understanding of the Fourteenth Amendment's framers.

Prior to 1939 the response to Black's independence was not heartening. Suggesting the uneasiness of the Court's liberals, Stone wrote privately that he was "really startled" by Black's "revolutionary dissents." Suggesting that one such opinion was the "handiwork of someone other than the nominal author," Stone declared that his new colleague needed "guidance from someone who is more familiar with the workings of the judicial process." Otherwise, Stone was "fearful" that Black would "not avoid the danger of frittering away his opportunity for judicial effectiveness by lack of good technique and by the desire to express ideas which, however valuable they may be in themselves, are irrelevant or untimely."

Black's willingness to "remake the Constitution *ab initio,*" or to use the "judicial opinion as a political tract," so concerned Stone that he confided his fears to journalist Marquis Childs. Childs then wrote a widely publicized article expressing grave doubts about Roosevelt's appointee. "Court-packing based on political partisanship," Childs exclaimed solemnly, "is no enduring cure for the old evil of deciding cases according to economic predilections," particularly by one "who has no judicial experience and only a comparatively limited legal experience." Basically the Stone/Childs criticism reflected a fear of going too far. Indeed, the article stirred a thorough debate regarding Black's individual abilities and the degree to which he symbolized Roosevelt's attempt to shape the Court. The justice's defenders retorted that he had "legal training enough" but that he needed "a course in hallowed platitudes." According to Yale Law School professor Walton Hamilton, the attack upon Black arose because "he regards the sacred cows as ordinary heifers." Black himself was unperturbed by the controversy.

The conflict aroused by Childs' article pointed up the deep strains among the liberal justices. A clear majority supported the reinterpretation of the Constitution's commerce clause and other provisions to overcome the problems created by the Great Depression. Once launched upon a constitutional revolution, however, the liberals could not agree on how far to go or the best way to get there. Stone's criticism of Black arose from the conviction that change was best achieved through skillful and reasonable alteration of established rules. He relied on craftsmanship to obscure the wholesale rewriting of doctrine. Black was more willing to return to first principles in order to fashion broadly based new constitutional interpretations. He looked beyond the narrow technical issue to the result. He saw the "social point of a case, its implications to the lives of people, in a flash." He then had the "energy and the ability to devise ways—new ways if need be—of serving what in his conception is the largest good."

The division among the liberals reflected still further disagreement over the limits of self-restraint. Once the Court gave general constitutional sanction to enlarged federal power, it confronted the problem of how far courts should exercise discretion in interpreting the meaning of legislative and administrative measures. Black favored a more complete deference to lawmakers than did Stone and his liberal colleagues. At one point during this period, Black wrote concurring in the results by disagreeing with the reasoning used to reach the outcome. The Court had resorted to its own analysis of the evidence rather than merely relying on a literal reading of the law. That such controversy should follow in the wake of the dramatic affirmation of the National Labor Relations Act and the Social Security Act in 1937 troubled liberal commentators.

The Court's pathbreaking approach to civil rights under the Fourteenth Amendment similarly raised various issues. Since the *Plessy* v. *Ferguson* decision of 1896 the Court had interpreted the Fourteenth Amendment's guarantee of equal protection of the laws in terms of the separate-but-equal doctrine. States could allow discrimination based on race as long as equal facilities or access were provided. Relying on this reading southern states had imposed racial segregation throughout the entire society.

The Court rarely looked beyond the language of the laws to determine whether in fact there was equality in the application of the separate-but-equal doctrine until 1938, when it considered *Missouri ex rel. Gaines* v. *Canada*. Missouri had complied with *Plessy* by providing tuition for blacks to attend law school in another state because they were excluded from attending its own law school. Was such an arrangement consistent with the equal protection clause of the Fourteenth Amendment? The Court, with Black joining a majority of 7 to 2, held that Missouri's policy violated the equal protection clause. This was a vigorous exercise of judicial activism.

By what standard did the Court justify such activism? In what became a much-cited passage, Footnote Number Four of *U.S.* v. *Carolene Products Co.* (1938), Stone suggested an answer. His opinion stressed that courts should defer to legislators and administrators in economic regulation. "Regulatory legislation affecting ordinary commercial transactions," Stone said, was "not to be pronounced unconstitutional" in most cases so long as it rested on some rational basis within the knowledge and experience of legislators. However, he recognized in Footnote Four that judges must scrutinize carefully statutes "directed at particular" religious, ethnic, or racial "discrete and insular minorities," to determine whether prejudice as a "special condition" interfered with the operation of democratic processes ordinarily relied on to protect minorities.

Although Black voted for racial justice in *Gaines,* he rejected Stone's Footnote Four formula. Stone's sanction of activism to protect "insular minorities" did not trouble Black, who soon thereafter wrote the opinion for a unanimous Court in *Pierre* v. *Louisiana,* reversing a murder verdict against a black man because the state had systematically and intentionally excluded blacks from local juries. The *Pierre* decision departed from decades of precedents in which the Court had deferred to southern officials in the application of the Fourteenth Amendment's equal protection guarantees. Yet Black opposed Footnote Four because it failed to establish adequate guidelines circumscribing the judges' discretion as to when activism was preferable to restraint. Black accepted the need for its limitation by courts only when the scope of judicial intervention was clearly prescribed. In cases involving racial discrimination imposed by state action, he wished the Court to rely on the intent of the framers of the Fourteenth Amendment's equal protection clause.

When the Court overturned state restrictions on individual liberty as contrary to the Fourteenth Amendment due process clause, Black accepted the theory that Justice Cardozo pronounced in *Palko* v. *Connecticut,* holding that certain rights guaranteed in the Constitution's Bill of Rights had—through "a process of absorption"—become part of the due process clause of the Fourteenth Amendment. Some rights were more significant than others, and only those "implicit in the concept of ordered liberty" were incorporated by the due process clause. Cardozo stressed that these rights were on a "different plane of social and moral values." He noted particularly the guarantees of free speech and press in the First Amendment, which constituted the "matrix, the indisputable condition for nearly every other freedom." At the same time he rejected the contention raised in the *Palko* case itself that the Fifth Amendment's proscription of double jeopardy was a fundamental right. Otherwise, Cardozo did not attempt to categorize which provisions applied to the states through the due process clause and which did not.

The Court's struggle to reconcile judicial activism and self-restraint did not involve some philosophical theory, but an effort to defer to Congress and state legislatures in economic and social policymaking, while establishing the presumption in favor of individual rights where states interfered with the Fourteenth Amendment's guarantees of equal protection or due process. Black had little problem exercising self-restraint toward federal or state economic policies that reflected the nation's overwhelming support of Roosevelt's liberalism. Similarly, the Court's activist defense of equal rights also was generally consistent with Black's principles. Black more than other justices, however, sought to establish specific guidelines limiting judicial discretion. To escape the discretionary vagueness implicit in Stone's Footnote Four, Black advocated following Cardozo's *Palko* theory.

By 1941 Roosevelt had entirely reconstituted the Court. Less than a year after Black's appointment, the President chose Solicitor General Stanley F. Reed after Justice Sutherland retired in 1938. Within a year Frankfurter and the forty-one-year-old chairman of the Securities and Exchange Commission, William O. Douglas, replaced Cardozo, who died, and Brandeis, who retired. In February 1940 Butler resigned, and former Michigan governor and U.S. Attorney General Frank Murphy took his seat. A year later Chief Justice Hughes and Justice McReynolds resigned and South Carolina Democrat James F. Byrnes and Attorney General Robert H. Jackson took their places. At the same time, Roosevelt promoted Stone from Associate to Chief Justice.

The change was apparent in *U.S.* v. *Darby*: the Court unanimously upheld the Fair Labor Standards Act. Stone's decision declared that under the commerce clause Congress possessed the authority to establish minimum wages and maximum hours for employees who produced goods for interstate trade. *Darby* undoubtedly gratified Black, whose dogged support of the Thirty-hour Week Bill had paved the way for the Fair Labor Standards Act. The unanimous consent given Stone's opinion suggested the extent to which Roosevelt had succeeded in altering the Court. He had appointed seven justices, each a sound New Deal liberal. Only Roberts and Stone remained from the earlier Court.

As the complexion of the Court changed, Black's influence grew. His dissents in the NLRB cases now became the Court's majority position. Black was also with the majority in upholding the second Agricultural Adjustment Act, which permitted full federal control of the nation's agricultural production. In other commerce clause issues Black's influence was less direct, though no less important. On the general use of the commerce power to expand federal authority, Black and his fellow liberals agreed.

In the field of civil rights Black's role was also significant. Beginning with the *Pierre* case, Hughes assigned him opinions upholding the rights of southern blacks because of the "unfortunate controversy" at the time of his appointment involving membership in the Ku Klux Klan. Indeed, after the *Gaines* decision the black press singled out Justice Black for praise even though he had not written the opinion. "A proven member of the Ku Klux Klan, Mr. Black now reverses himself," noted an editorial in the *Nashville-Globe-Independent,* "and approves the decision of the Court to compel" the University of Missouri Law School to "admit Negroes." Black received letters from Walter White, secretary of the NAACP, commending him for his stands in *Gaines* and *Pierre.*

Black's opinion for a unanimous Court in *Chambers* v. *Florida* (1940) was perhaps his most ringing defense of racial justice. The case involved a jury's murder verdicts based on confessions coerced from four young black tenant farmers. Local law enforcement officials had arrested the youths without a warrant, held them in jail without formal charges or an opportunity to consult counsel, and subjected them to nearly a week of questioning during late night sessions. Throughout the period the four also faced continuous danger of mob violence. As a result they finally admitted to having committed the crimes.

The case received national media attention. The constitutional issue in *Chambers* transcended the injustices evident in the facts. The only ground on which Black and his colleagues could challenge a jury verdict in a Florida court was to hold that the coerced confessions violated the due process clause of the Fourteenth Amendment. In the *Palko* case, the Court had already announced that the due process clause comprehended certain rights guaranteed in the Bill of Rights. However, the Court had not considered whether the Fifth Amendment's protection against self-incrimination was among those rights.

Black's decision answered this question. The "testimony of centuries, in governments of varying kinds of populations of different races and beliefs, stood as proof that physical and mental torture and coercion" had resulted in "tragically unjust sacrifices." The "rack, the thumbscrew, the wheel, solitary confinement, protracted questioning and cross-questioning" entrapped the "helpless or unpopular." Those suffering most from "secret and dictatorial proceedings have almost always been the poor, the ignorant, the numerically weak, the friendless, and the powerless." Against such evils, Black concluded, "fundamental standards of procedure in criminal trials" were "made operative against the States by the Fourteenth Amendment." As a result, no "higher duty, no more solemn responsibility, rests upon this Court than that of translating into living law and maintaining the constitutional shield deliberately planned and inscribed for the benefit of every human being subject to our Constitution—of whatever race, creed, or persuasion."

Although Frankfurter joined the majority in the case, he opposed Black's view of the broader relationship between the Bill of Rights and the due process clause. The two justices disagreed, wrote Frankfurter, over the "criteria of selection as to the nine Amendments—which applies and which does not apply." He opposed wide-ranging "judicial legislation" based on the sort of independent judgment that had been overturned in the *Erie* opinion, but he also rejected the "opposite extreme of wishing all law to be formulated by legislation." For Frankfurter, it was the "everlasting problem of how far is too far and how much is too much. Judges," he reminded Black, "cannot escape the responsibility of filling in gaps which the finitude of even the most imaginative legislation renders inevitable." Thus the issue was "not whether the judges make law, but when and how and how much." Finally, Frankfurter warned Black of "the evil of a lack of candor. By covering up the lawmaking function of judges, we miseducate the people and fail to bring out into the open the real responsibility of judges for what they do, leaving it to the primary lawmaking agency, the legislature, to correct what judges do if they don't like it."

U.S. v. *Classic* (1941) suggested even subtler divisions among the justices. The case raised the issue whether the federal government could lawfully regulate a state primary election integral to the process of selecting candidates for federal office. In this case the evidence revealed that ballot-box tampering by state officials in the city of New Orleans had resulted in the exclusion of blacks from voting. Stone's majority opinion distinguished the case from numerous contrary precedents holding federal intervention lawful to prevent corruption in national elections. However, Justice Douglas, joined by Black and Murphy, dissented. They "agreed with most of the views expressed in the opinion" but argued that Stone had neglected to take into account the rights of those accused of obstructing the electoral process. "Civil liberties are too dear," Douglas asserted, "to permit conviction for crimes which are only implied."

The application of First Amendment guarantees to the states through the due process clause was also divisive. The Court overturned city ordinances requiring permits before workers could conduct public meetings and similar laws restricting the distribution of religious literature. In the *Gobitis* case of 1940, however, the Court voted 8 to 1 to uphold the authority of a Pennsylvania school board to expel children who refused to salute the American flag. The children claimed that, as Jehovah's Witnesses, they viewed the flag salute as a form of idolatry prohibited by their faith. Frankfurter held that the school board's ceremony was vital to fostering patriotism, "the basis of national security," and as such was an "interest inferior to none in the hierarchy of legal values," not even inferior to religious freedom.

The lone dissenter was Stone. He urged that the "right of the individual to hold such opinions as he will and to give them reasonable free expression" was as vital to democracy as the Constitution's sanction of majority rule. As a result, the state's authority to demand patriotic deference did not "outweigh the freedom from compulsory violation of religious faith which has been thought worthy of constitutional protection." Frankfurter was surprised that Stone departed from the most reasonable reading of Footnote Number Four. Personal freedom was best maintained so long as the democratic process remained open and unobstructed and not enforced against popular policy by the coercion of unelected judges.

Black's strongest challenge to the Court's stance on free expression involved picketing. Beginning in 1937, the Court held peaceful picketing to be a form of speech protected from state interference under the First and Fourteenth amendments. However, in *Milk Wagon Drivers Union* v. *Meadowmoor Dairies* (1941) Frankfurter wrote for the majority that a state court could issue an injunction to prevent picketing when it was marred by the destruction of property and other disorder. Black adamantly rejected Frankfurter's opinion. He stressed that only a few demonstrators had actually engaged in violence, and it was "going a long way" because of these few to deny six thousand other members of their union "the right to express their opinion." He then articulated a broader guarantee for free expression than Cardozo had implied in *Palko*: "I view the guarantees of the First Amendment as the foundation upon which our government rests and without which it could not continue to endure as conceived and planned." For Black, "Freedom to speak and to write about public questions was as important as the heart to the human body." If that "heart be weakened, the result is debilitation; if it be stilled, the result is death."

Values rooted in Black's past shaped his attempt to balance the judicial role, majority rule, and individual liberty. In the

NLRB and commerce clause cases he favored judicial restraint, supporting New Deal regulation. Sensitive to the tenuous interdependency of community welfare and individual rights, however, he also upheld judicial intervention against the states under the Fourteenth Amendment. Despite Black's faith in the jury, his experience in Birmingham had demonstrated that blacks and ethnic minorities often suffered at the hands of white jurors. As a result, in *Pierre* and *Chambers* Black for the first time extended to citizens in state trials several Bill of Rights guarantees applied through the due process clause. The results were consistent with long-held convictions.

The same values guided his effort to set appropriate limits for judicial interference with the popular will. In *Gaines* he voted for the first significant restriction of racial segregation under the *Plessy* doctrine. In the *Classic* case, however, Black joined Douglas's dissent, refusing to support voting rights at the cost of weakening the rights of criminal defendants. A citizen's right to participate in a free, untainted federal election process did not outweigh another citizen's right to be governed by clear and fair criminal laws. Both urged Congress rather than the Court to intervene by enacting legislation that would both prevent corrupt elections and preserve criminal due process.

Black's most difficult challenge, however, involved the extent of free expression protected under the First and Fourteenth amendments. In the *Palko* decision he favored the proposition that the First Amendment's guarantees of free speech and press were among those "fundamental principles" undoubtedly "absorbed" into the due process clause. Yet Black believed judges should prevent legislative interference with some, but not all, individual expression, the power itself being subject to restrictions. From close association with both organized labor and religious organizations throughout his public career, Black considered free assembly, peaceful picketing, and solicitation as vital to "ordered liberty." Accordingly, in cases involving the worker's right to assemble and picket, as well as a religious group's right to peddle its literature, community liberty gave way to individual liberty. But freedom of conscience, the issue raised in *Gobitis,* did not receive such protection. Certain policies or symbols such as prohibition or a flag salute were so essential to community welfare, Black believed, that private considerations of personal faith were of secondary importance.

By the end of 1941 both success and failure characterized Roosevelt's influence on the Court. As the justices who had confronted the constitutional transformation of 1936–37 retired, Roosevelt had replaced them with loyal New Deal liberals. The Court, as a result, had increasingly deferred to Congress, and to a lesser extent to state legislatures, in the field of economic regulation. This exercise of restraint raised anew the dilemma of whether the benefits of big government outweighed its costs. After 1939 the issue arose most conspicuously in connection with racial and religious minorities and organized labor. In response, the Court began to take a more activist approach to civil liberties, applying selective provisions of the Bill of Rights to overturn state laws as violations of the due process clause of the Fourteenth Amendment. The resulting tension between activism and self-restraint, however, aroused new conflict over the limits of judicial discretion. The disagreement among Black, Stone, and Frankfurter reflected contrary readings of the constitutional principles established from 1937 on. More fundamentally, the question was how far the Court should go in subordinating majoritarian to individual rights. Then on December 7, 1941, the Japanese attack on Pearl Harbor subsumed the liberals' dilemma in a world at war.

CHAPTER SIX

Justice at War (1941–1945)

Black and his colleagues were near the center of struggles involving the federal government's wartime constitutional authority. Immediately after Pearl Harbor Roosevelt asked Congress for broad authority to mobilize the nation against the Axis powers. Congress established new bureaucracies such as the Office of Price Administration, while Roosevelt pushed his constitutional prerogatives as commander in chief to the hilt. At one point he even threatened not to enforce a law, thereby forcing Congress to repeal it and pass another he favored. From 1937 to 1941 the Court had sustained the creation of enlarged federal authority to overcome the Great Depression. In the name of "wartime necessity" Black and his fellow justices continued this policy of deference.

The growth of executive power resulted in a more aggressive Congress. The war's demands for military personnel and expanding economic production ended the Depression. They also prevented the revival of social policies suspended since passage of the Fair Labor Standards Act of 1938. Roosevelt justified this continued cessation of welfare programs on the ground that "Dr. New Deal must give way to Dr. Win the War." Roosevelt accepted the erosion of New Deal liberalism in part because in 1942 Republicans won 47 House and 10 Senate seats, gains that gave the conservative coalition of southern Democrats and Republicans new clout. By 1943 Congress passed, over Roosevelt's veto, the War Labor Disputes Act, requiring unions to wait thirty days before striking and empowering the President to seize businesses embroiled in strikes. Finally, the Allied military effort and concurrent negotiations compelled the subordination of domestic to international policymaking from Pearl Harbor through the President's fourth-term reelection in 1944 to his death in April 1945, and to the war's end the following August.

The Court's restraint toward wartime big government paralleled increased activism in the sphere of civil liberties—except in cases arising from the conduct of the war. Prior to Pearl Harbor, American fascist groups had pushed a campaign of ethnic, racial, and religious bigotry, drawing on the same sentiments that had spawned the Klan and the Scottsboro controversy. Once the United States entered the war, however, the public resisted attitudes so closely identified with Adolf Hitler. In particular there was mounting criticism of the South's racial segregation, set off by the favorable reception given Gunnar Myrdal's critical examination of race relations, *An American Dilemma.* Moreover, waves of southern blacks moved to northern industrial centers seeking wartime jobs and thereby creating new voting blocs that supported racial justice. Black labor leader A. Philip Randolph furthered that cause by pressuring Roosevelt to establish a Fair Employment Practices Commission.

The Court's decisions reflected these changes. Through the due process clause of the Fourteenth Amendment it applied First Amendment guarantees to overturn state restrictions of free expression and religion. At the same time the Court revitalized the Fifteenth Amendment's protection of black voting rights, dormant since the collapse of Reconstruction. As the Court grappled with these issues, Black struggled to fashion a distinctive constitutional theory that would reconcile individual rights with community welfare.

Other conflicts also shaped Black's role on the Court. Roosevelt's appointment of Wiley B. Rutledge to replace James F. Byrnes, who resigned to head a defense agency in 1942, established a new mix of personal relations. Despite the "war, things move along here more or less as usual," he wrote to Harold Laski, an old friend. The work load was "very heavy, both in number and importance of the cases. So far as I am concerned, this only serves to make the job more interesting." He did not mention, however, the pronounced divisions among Roosevelt's liberal justices, as indicated by the precipitous growth in the number of dissenting opinions. During the Court's 1940 term there were 110 dissents; the number rose in 1941 to 158, in 1942 to 165, in 1943 to 186, and in 1944 to 231.

Black's most controversial decision involving individual rights and wartime necessity arose from the internment of Japanese-Americans. Pearl Harbor revived decades-old fears among West Coast whites of a "Yellow Peril," focusing now on people of Japanese ancestry living in California, Oregon, and Washington. Approximately one-third of these 112,000 residents were elderly aliens who, though born in Japan, had lived in the United States nearly their entire lives but had been denied citizenship by a 1924 law. The remaining two-thirds were American-born, second-generation residents possessing full citizenship. Business and labor groups joined what West Coast military commander General John L. DeWitt described as "a tremendous volume of public opinion now developing against the Japanese." According to General DeWitt, the "best people of California," including Governor Culbert Olson and state Attorney General Earl Warren, shared the conviction voiced by one subordinate that "their racial characteristics are such that we cannot understand or trust even the citizen Japanese." General DeWitt summed up the popular racial view equating Japanese Americans with the enemy: "A Jap's a Jap."

Following the request of War Department officials, Roosevelt signed in February 1942 an executive order granting military authorities the power to designate areas from which to exclude "any or all persons." A month later Congress enacted legislation making violation of any such military order a federal crime punishable by imprisonment for up to one year. As a result, General DeWitt and his subordinates imposed a curfew from 5 P.M. to 6 A.M. upon all Japanese-Americans. At the same time, they issued over 100 "exclusion orders," requiring Japanese-Americans to dispose of their property within a week, leave their businesses and residences, and report immediately to "assembly centers" with only those possessions they could carry in their arms. From the assembly areas, armed guards accompanied the Japanese-Americans to "relocation centers" situated in isolated areas from California to Arkansas. Those centers were, in fact, detention camps operated by the War Relocation Authority. There, thousands of American citizens lived for as long as four years, even though they were neither charged with nor convicted of any crime.

This wholesale denial of constitutional rights came before the Court during the summer of 1943 in *Hirabayashi* v. *U.S.* Gordon Hirabayashi, a U.S. citizen and Quaker pacifist attending the University of Washington, opposed the curfew and the exclusion order as contrary to the "democratic principles for which this nation lives." His lawyers argued that General DeWitt's orders violated the Fifth Amendment's due process clause and were motivated by racial antagonism, not military necessity. The government claimed that the orders were a reasonable response to a "serious threat" of Japanese attack, and that the Japanese-American population included "a number of persons who might assist the enemy" if such an attack occurred. Black joined a unanimous opinion written by Stone. Declining even to consider whether the relocation program was constitutional, the chief justice upheld the legality of the curfew. Declining to question the "wisdom" of those upon whom the Constitution placed the responsibility of warmaking, Stone conceded that legal distinctions "between citizens solely because of their ancestry" were "odious to a free people," but he, nevertheless, recognized the government's right to "place citizens of one ancestry in a different category from others," if they were "a greater source of danger than those of a different ancestry."

Despite the unanimity of the *Hirabayashi* decision, the justices were in fact divided. Stone's acceptance of racial classifications so disturbed Murphy that he wrote and circulated a lengthy dissent, which Frankfurter eventually convinced him to publish as a concurrence. Douglas, in his concurrence, emphasized that Stone's decision applied only to the curfew and did not address the lawfulness of the detention and relocation policies. Jackson and Roberts remained silent, but had doubts about the government's claim that the Japanese-Americans might be a military threat. Black, Frankfurter, Reed, and Rutledge declined to consider the broader implications of Stone's opinion.

By 1944, however, members of the Court had changed their minds. *Ex parte Endo* questioned the continued confinement of the Japanese-Americans in detention camps. The government conceded that Congress had never formally authorized the indefinite detention of loyal Japanese-Americans, including the eighteen-year-old U.S. citizen Mitsuye Endo. Accordingly, Douglas for a unanimous Court (including Black) held that Endo was entitled to a writ of habeas corpus freeing her from a relocation camp. Although Douglas's decision prompted the dismantling of the camps, it ignored altogether the larger issue of whether the detention itself was unconstitutional. Moreover, Douglas did not discuss whether the Constitution permitted the forcible holding of American citizens charged with no crime far away from any combat zone under military orders.

On the same day the Court unanimously decided *Endo*, it divided in *Korematsu* v. *U.S.* Citizen Fred Korematsu had stayed in California in order to remain with his fiancee. Upon his arrest, he argued that the government's policies violated the due process clause of the Fifth Amendment, particularly because compliance with the exclusion order would inevitably have led to confinement in a detention center, which the Court had just struck down in cases involving loyal citizens. Indeed, Justice Department officials had suppressed evidence discovered by the FBI and military intelligence showing irrefutably that all but a handful of the Japanese-Americans were loyal. Had this evidence been publicized it would have undermined the government's claim that "wartime necessity" justified the exclusion program.

Without such proof, however, Black for the majority deferred to the military's judgment. He accepted with little question the government's argument that the Japanese-Americans as a group posed a potential threat. Black admitted that the exclusion worked hardships upon loyal citizens, but, he said, "hardships are a part of war and war is an aggregation of hardships." Like Douglas in *Endo,* Black also declined to consider the constitutionality of the detention policy.

Justices Murphy, Jackson, and Roberts dissented. Murphy declared that the unquestioning acceptance of military judgment went "over the very brink of constitutional power and falls into the ugly abyss of racism." He rejected Black's deference to a policy that amounted to the "legalization of racism." Jackson warned that this exercise of judicial restraint established the precedent of group guilt resting like a "loaded weapon ready for the hand of any authority that can bring forward a plausible claim of an urgent need." Roberts rejected Black's separation of the exclusion orders from the relocation and detention policies, arguing that it ignored the degree to which Korematsu, "solely because of his ancestry," was caught in a "cleverly devised trap to accomplish the real purpose of the military authority, which was to lock him up in a concentration camp."

Black, however, viewed the Japanese-Americans' internment in terms of the wartime struggle for democracy. Black looked on the federal government's program not as an issue of individual rights. Instead, it represented the continuing tension between individual liberty and community welfare, and in this case war required the subordination of the minority to the majority. At the same time, however, the government's deliberate suppression of evidence demonstrating the loyalty of the Japanese-Americans revealed the wisdom of the dissenting justices' rejection of Black's *Korematsu* decision. The people no less than a dictator would abuse their power unless checked by constitutional limitations.

A case involving the civil liberties of German saboteurs raised related issues. During the summer of 1942, a band of German military personnel, equipped to sabotage various war industries, landed from submarines in the United States. They were soon captured, and Roosevelt ordered them tried before a special military tribunal for violating the laws of war. At the same time the President excluded them from all civilian courts, an action questioned by the U.S. Army colonels charged with the Germans' defense. Shortly after the Civil War, in *ex parte Milligan,* the Court had held that military trials of civilians were unconstitutional in areas remote from actual hostilities and where civilian courts operated. According to the laws of war the saboteurs were clearly military personnel. Nonetheless, the defense counsels were concerned about the bearing of *Milligan* on the lawfulness of the defendants' detention and trial by a military rather than a civilian tribunal. The lawyers arranged a meeting with administration officials and justices Roberts and Black to consider bringing the question before the Supreme Court. As a result, for the first time in twenty-two years, the Court interrupted its summer recess in order to decide whether the prisoners could seek release through a writ of habeas corpus.

Black expressed his views in a letter to Stone. Black did not want to "destroy the protections declared by the *Milligan* case." Consequently, he desired to go "no further than to declare that these particular defendants are subject to the jurisdiction of a military tribunal because of the circumstances and purposes of their entry into this country as a part of the enemy's war forces." This limitation "would leave the *Milligan* doctrine untouched." Stone accepted these points in the decision for a unanimous Court. The constitutional law of the United States traditionally recognized that American military tribunals were not courts within the meaning of the Constitution, the chief justice said. It was therefore illogical to argue that the same Constitution that withheld certain due process rights from United States servicemen nonetheless sanctioned those rights for the military personnel of an enemy nation. Stone also asserted that the warmaking power provided Roosevelt with sufficient authority to establish the special military court. Finally, Stone held that under the laws of war the tribunal was justified in ordering the saboteurs' execution.

The German saboteurs raised another conflict between wartime necessity and civil liberties. Anthony Cramer, a naturalized American citizen of German background, had met and conversed with two of the saboteurs prior to their arrest. FBI agents witnessed Cramer's actions, and he was tried and convicted for having committed treason. Under Article III, section 3, conviction for treason required the performance of an "overt act" either confessed to in open court or observed by two witnesses. The issue was whether Cramer's amiable relationship with his nation's enemies was an "overt act" within the meaning of the Constitution. Jackson for a 5 to 4 majority overturned the conviction, holding that neither Cramer's conduct itself nor other evidence revealed an intent to commit treason. Douglas's dissenting opinion followed closely the logic Black had set out in a note explaining his decision to join the minority. After a careful examination of the record against Cramer, Black wrote, "if a conviction is not to be sustained on evidence such as the Government produced here, I doubt if there could be many conviction for treason unless American citizens were actually found in the Army of the enemy." In light of evidence, Black concluded that the "jury's verdict was justified."

In the saboteur and Cramer cases, Black further refined his view toward individual liberty. He believed that personal freedom was not an end in itself; but facilitated the democratic self-government on which community welfare depended. So far as Black was concerned, anyone affiliated with the enemy possessed only the most elemental due process rights. Thus as an American citizen Cramer had a constitutional right to a jury trial. The saboteurs, on the other hand, had only those rights existing under the laws of war. In either case, however, wartime exigencies made community security the paramount value. Black's dissenting vote in *Cramer* demonstrated that he was less willing than other justices to broaden the civil liberties of the nation's enemies.

Personality clashes encourage petty disputes among the justices. When Roberts retried in 1945 six justices refused to sign a letter commemorating the occasion if it included any reference to "regret" that he was leaving or the statement that he had made "fidelity to principle" his "guide to decision." Suggesting a deep aversion to any endorsement of Roberts's performance as a justice, Black led the opposition. Jackson, however, joined by Frankfurter and Stone, refused to sign a letter "that deliberately omits the only sentence that credits [Roberts] with good motives." Finally, the justice received no letter at all. Chief Justice Stone merely announced the retirement by reading a text that omitted the phrases that Black and the others had rejected.

Meanwhile, the growing popular opposition to organized labor divided the Court. In 1944 and 1945 the justices considered in several related cases the question whether the Fair Labor Standards Act bound coal companies to pay miners for travel time between the mine portal and the place where digging actually commenced. Although the Act included no such specific obligation, Justice Murphy for a 5–4 majority interpreted the law broadly in favor of the miners. Jackson led dissenters Frankfurter, Roberts, and Stone, arguing that Congress had not intended such a liberal construction of the FLSA. Had Black not voted for Murphy's opinion the resulting 4 to 4 deadlock would have prevented a decision. This angered Jackson because Black's former law partner was the miners' attorney, a consideration which suggested to him that Black should have withdrawn from the cases. Indeed one of the employers, the Jewell Ridge Coal Corporation, petitioned the Court for a rehearing because of the personal connection. The Court denied the petition, but Jackson remained convinced that Black had acted improperly.

The justices were more united on other regulatory issues. Beginning in 1937 the Court had significantly expanded the scope of federal regulation under the commerce clause; it subsequently viewed the trend as consistent with federal management of a wartime economy. In *Wickard* v. *Filburn* (1942) it unanimously upheld provisions of the Agricultural Adjustment Act whereby Congress delegated to the Secretary of Agriculture the power to impose marketing quotas on wheat, even on that grown and consumed locally. Jackson's opinion admitted that such production rarely if ever directly touched the flow of interstate commerce, but local use of the staple did affect nationwide commodity prices. Accordingly, federal regulation was valid under the commerce power.

Disputes also arose out of disagreements over state control of civil rights. Roberts in *Grovey* v. *Townsend* (1935) had main-

tained that southern primaries that prohibited blacks from voting did not violate the Fifteenth Amendment. He held that the Amendment did not apply to private political activities such as the Democratic party's primary. In 1944, when the Court in *Smith* v. *Allright* specifically reversed *Grovey,* Roberts dissented. Justice Reed, speaking for eight members, held that white primaries were so fundamental to the selection of candidates in all southern elections that they were in fact state action, not private. Roberts responded that the Court's policy of freely disregarding "considered decisions" indicated an "intolerance for what those who have composed this court in the past have conscientiously and deliberately concluded."

In *Smith* v. *Allright* the justices also confronted another face of prejudice: anti-Semitism. Once the Court agreed in conference to overrule *Grovey,* Stone assigned the writing of the decision to Frankfurter, but Jackson raised the issue that resulted in Stone's reassigning the opinion. You are not a Southerner and "you are a Jew," Jackson told Frankfurter, and because a lot of "people are bent on exploiting anti-Semitism, as you well know, I do not think that they ought to be given needless materials." Frankfurter then discussed the matter with Chief Justice Stone, who decided against asking Black to write because no one knew "what [he] would do to it." The chief justice turned the opinion over to Stanley Reed of Kentucky.

Hugo, Jr.'s military service provided Black with another perspective on the sort of racial and religious prejudice the Court confronted. A letter recounted a brutal attack by white enlisted men on a black noncommissioned officer because he had used the same restroom as the whites. "I got down there and tried to drag him out of their way, and stop the bleeding a little bit. I could tell most everybody had contempt for me," he wrote his father. When the M.P.s came, they "didn't even ask who had hit him or what had happened to him. All they could say was: 'Somebody sure coldcocked themselves a nigger.'" Black's response reflected his own experience and understanding of human nature. You were "bound to be disturbed by the innate or cultivated cruelty of the soldiers who ruthlessly attacked another soldier simply because of his color,"

he said. "If you live long enough, you will see many more evidences of cruel propensities in individuals. You will not find that such characteristics can be chalked up wholly against any one race group or class." Moreover, Black assured his son, "Racial intolerance as a rule rests on egotism, or a concealed inferiority complex."

The justice did recount his son's experience to convince others. One evening, the "son of an active New Jersey Republican," who had "inherited some of the prejudicial views against non-Gentiles, particularly Jewish people," visited the Black home. As Black wrote to Hugo, Jr., "Your vivid picture of the hates of the varied groups in Camp proved to be about the best argument I could make to him . . . he left my house with a completely changed attitude."

A confrontation between Black and Frankfurter had further implications for the states' control of individual rights. Frankfurter favored following doctrines inherited from the English common law, which gave a comparatively restrictive interpretation of the First Amendment. Black, however, supported permitting more, rather than less, freedom of expression. This issue arose in *Bridges* v. *California* (1941). A state court had convicted labor radical Harry Bridges and the editors of the *Los Angeles Times* for publishing criticism of trials arising from labor unrest. On the day after Pearl Harbor, Black announced the opinion for a Court that split 5–4, Frankfurter, Roberts, Stone, and Byrnes in dissent. Denying that the published criticism posed a clear and present danger, Black struck down the convictions as a violation of the First and Fourteenth amendments.

Black's decision was a dramatic shift by the Court. When the case was argued initially in 1940 Frankfurter was assigned to write for the majority upholding the convictions of Bridges and the newspaper editors. Black led the dissenters. As Frankfurter circulated drafts of his opinion he developed the idea that "the power exerted by the courts of California is deeply rooted in the system of administering justice evolved by liberty-loving English-speaking peoples." In the draft of his dissent, Black argued on the contrary that his personal study of the origins of the First Amendment revealed that no "purpose in ratifying the

Bill of Rights was much clearer than that of securing for the people of the United States much greater freedom of religion, expression, assembly, and petition than the people of Great Britain had ever enjoyed." He further attempted to emphasize, citing Jefferson, why the Court should encourage rather than restrict free expression. "First in the catalogue of human liberties essential to the life and growth of a government of, for, and by the people are those liberties written into the First Amendment to our Constitution. They are the pillars upon which popular government rests and without which a government of free men cannot survive."

By 1941, however, the relative position of the two justices had been reversed, so that Black was writing for the majority and Frankfurter for the minority. Although the immediate reasons for the Court's change were known only to the justices themselves, it gained momentum during the war. In the *Gobitis* decision of 1940 Frankfurter had rejected the claim of Jehovah's Witnesses that the Fourteenth and First amendments exempted their children from Pennsylvania's mandatory flag salute. Black went along with Frankfurter's opinion because he agreed that the salute was vital to community unity during a time of growing world struggle. But as Hitler justified authoritarian government and conquest in terms of racial superiority, Black and other justices perceived the need to reconsider their stance toward individual rights. Indeed, the connection between Nazism and prejudice deeply troubled Black. He owned and studied Hitler's *Mein Kampf,* and he saw Germany's aggression as an example of unchecked power stifling individual freedom. The Nazis' persecutions of ethnic and racial minorities and political dissenters were "simply a repetition of the course of history when people get too much power."

After the war began, the Jehovah's Witnesses continued to challenge state-imposed restrictions. In 1942 the Court upheld city ordinances in Arkansas and Alabama requiring the religious group to pay a tax in order to sell denominational literature in local communities. Four justices dissented, including Black and Douglas, who specifically repudiated their votes in *Gobitis*: "this is an appropriate occasion to state that we now

believed that [*Gobitis*] was wrongly decided." They were now "certain" that the "nation's democratic form of government, functioning under the historic Bill of Rights, has a high responsibility to accommodate itself to the religious views of minorities, however unpopular and unorthodox those views may be."

The following year the dissenters became a majority. In a case arising from Pennsylvania, the Jehovah's Witnesses asked the Court to reconsider the constitutionality of the municipal taxes. Douglas, writing for the majority that included Black, struck down the tax ordinances as violations of the First and Fourteenth amendments, and the Court went further in *West Virginia* v. *Barnette,* when Jackson, writing for a 6–3 majority, overruled *Gobitis*.

Black wrote a concurring opinion in the *Barnette* case. No "well-ordered society," he said, could permit individuals an "absolute right" of protection from state interference. Repudiating the reasoning of *Gobitis,* however, he said that neither "our domestic tranquility in peace nor our martial effort in war depend on compelling little children to participate in a ceremony which ends in nothing for them but a fear of spiritual condemnation." A compulsory "ceremonial" when "enforced against conscientious objectors" was "more likely to defeat than to serve its high purpose," and thus state laws should "permit the widest toleration of conflicting viewpoints consistent with a society of free men." Finally, he declared, "Words uttered under coercion are proof of loyalty to nothing but self-interest. Love of country must spring from willing hearts and free minds, inspired by a fair administration of wise laws enacted by the people's elected representatives within the bounds of express constitutional prohibitions."

Frankfurter thoroughly rejected the Court's overturning of his *Gobitis* opinion. "One who belongs to the most vilified and persecuted minority in history" could not oppose in principle the "general libertarian views" of the Court's opinion, he admitted. Such views offended, however, his even stronger commitment to restraint. It was vital that courts use the power to strike down state and federal laws sparingly, deferring in most cases to legislators, administrators, and chief executives.

In the *Barnette* case the issue was, he said, which of two claims should prevail: "that of a state to enact and enforce laws within its general competence or that of an individual to refuse obedience because of the demands of his conscience." The Court should have rejected activism in favor of restraint and upheld the majority interest over individual rights.

Frankfurter's dissent was part of a broader clash with Black over the due process clause. The *Palko* decision of 1937 and Stone's Footnote Four of 1938 had raised the issue of what standard should govern the status of the Bill of Rights' guarantees under the Fourteenth Amendment's due process clause. The chief justice's lone dissent in the first flag salute case and the Court's subsequent turnabout in its sequel revealed just how ambiguous the doctrines were. Meanwhile, in various early decisions Black had suggested that specific portions of the Bill of Rights were incorporated through the due process clause. According to this view, the judge's ability to protect individual freedom was both enlarged and restricted. If under the due process clause the judge was bound to apply the Bill of Rights to the states, his power was increased. At the same time this authority could not exceed what was literally prescribed in those same provisions.

Even those comprising the new activist majority, however, declined to accept Black's emerging theory of incorporation. Consequently, he did not publicly articulate it, though he came close to doing so in the footnote of a dissent in *Betts* v. *Brady*. The Court decided the case in 1942, at the very time Black and Douglas were disassociating themselves from their votes in *Gobitis*. For a majority Roberts held that the Sixth Amendment's guarantee of right to counsel did not apply to the states through the due process clause. Dissenter Black, joined by Douglas and Murphy, however, cited historical evidence showing that the "sponsors" of the Fourteenth Amendment in both the House and the Senate purposed "to make secure against invasion by the states the fundamental liberties and safeguards set out in the Bill of Rights."

Throughout this period Black and Frankfurter discussed the theory of incorporation. After his defeat in *Barnette*, Frankfurter wrote a lengthy memo explaining to Black why he questioned the Court's new activism in general and Black's idea in particular. Supporting the "right of a democracy to make mistakes and correct its errors by the organs that reflect popular will," he urged the Court to limit the "undemocratic feature" of the government by restricting its power to the "narrowest limits." Citing the pattern of "fluctuating majorities on this Court," Frankfurter asked which of the "nine Amendments are to be deemed incorporated and which are left out?" Black responded that the intentions of the framers of the due process clause could guide the Court in applying the incorporation theory. Unconvinced, Frankfurter exclaimed that the "War is for me meaningless and Hitler becomes the true prophet if there is no such thing as law different from and beyond the individuals who give it expression."

Resistance to Black's incorporation theory was part of the dispute regarding wartime self-restraint and activism. There was no agreement on the limits of judicial discretion, and most justices consistently supported neither Black's approach to activism nor Frankfurter's stand for restraint. The Court overruled state restrictions of civil liberty at the same time that it subordinated the rights of Japanese-Americans and saboteurs. It blended restraint and activism in sweeping away established precedents to uphold expanded federal economic regulation while preserving a modicum of state control. These inconsistencies arose from the inability of Roosevelt's liberal Court to reconcile enlarged federal power and individual liberty.

Throughout this period, Black also experienced difficulties in his personal life. In 1944 he wrote Harold Laski that after "four bad years" Mrs. Black had "almost completely recovered" from a major operation. "My two boys are in the Air Corps, though both, much to their regret," were "denied an opportunity for combat service because of physical defects—one asthma, and the other bad hearing." According to the elder Josephine, "not a month" passed without some "major crisis" in the Black family. Indeed it seemed as if they had "practically bought the George Washington University Hospital."

However, Black's unshakable convictions gave him strength. "So long as you do your duty" and "live so as to keep your own self-respect, and keep your head in the midst of temporary disappointments," he wrote Hugo, Jr., in 1944, "I shall be just as proud of you as though you occupied the shoes of General Eisenhower, himself." Nothing was "really disgraceful except that which is dishonorable and it is never dishonorable to fail to achieve something if the person does the best he can." It was essential also to appreciate the "many, many kind and gentle persons who try to make other people happy." He urged Hugo, Jr., to "be philosophical about what you see and hear, enter into no controversies for the single purpose of being controversial, and be as nice to everybody on all occasions (even those whose conduct you detest), as you would like for people to be to you." In April 1944, he wrote Sterling that there was "much evidence that while human progress is slow, it is nevertheless sure. While we may have a relapse at any time, I think that this country has during my lifetime moved in the direction of a better distribution of justice." Moreover, he observed, "from long experience in many governmental affairs, I have long since decided that [government] works about as well as anybody could expect, despite the petty political mistakes which crop up in the activities of those engaged in public service. Furthermore, I think we have a much better government than we had in 1789, and will have a still better one in 1989." Because human beings had many weaknesses, both physical and mental, societies composed of such individuals could not be expected to achieve perfection overnight.

Black's determination to implement these values shaped his contribution to wartime liberalism. He attempted to resolve the tensions between judicial activism and self-restraint by emphasizing the interdependence between community welfare as defined by majoritarian democracy and broad guarantees of personal freedom as defended by the courts. Adjusting the ever-shifting balance, the Court could, Black firmly believed, preserve and indeed strengthen New Deal liberalism. Black's *Korematsu* decision and the failure to win acceptance of the incorporation theory, however, reaffirmed the intractable nature of the liberal dilemma.

CHAPTER SEVEN

Cold War Liberalism (1945–1952)

❖
❖

New national security pressures after the war compelled Black to fight for greater constitutional limitations on government. The struggle over liberal principles arose amidst mounting popular fear of communist subversion that threatened both the rights of individuals and the welfare of the community. As the conflict engulfed Black's family and friends, he attempted to fashion clear prescriptions defining the constitutional boundary between individual liberty and governmental authority. Increasingly, however, the Court's preference for self-restraint threw him on the defensive.

Black had earlier campaigned for Missouri Senator Harry S Truman, who as President now confronted the new challenges in domestic and foreign affairs. Americans who had accepted Roosevelt's subordination of social-welfare policymaking to military necessity yearned for a return to the peacetime prosperity that had preceded the Great Depression. Black realized that significant international hostilities impinged upon Truman's ability to lead the United States toward this goal. The alliance with the Soviet Union had been essential to achieving victory over Hitler's Germany, but mutual distrust over numerous postwar issues destroyed cooperation. At the same time, although the monopoly of atomic weapons gave the United States military superiority, no western nation wanted war with the Soviet Union.

Domestic tensions also steadily increased. Though Congress established increased executive control of economic policymaking through the Council of Economic Advisors and enlarged the executive's peacetime authority to conduct military and counterintelligence operations, the President's domestic programs stalled. By the end of 1946 labor unrest, shortages, and inflation facilitated the first election of Republican congressional majorities since 1930. The most troubling defeat was passage of the Taft-Hartley Act over Truman's veto. The new law imposed restrictions on unions, enabled the President to order an injunction against any strike threatening the national security, and empowered him to initiate a "cooling off" period before a strike could begin. It also required union leaders to swear that they neither believed in communist teachings nor were members of communist political organizations.

Although southern Dixiecrats and radical Progressives deserted the Democrats, Truman was reelected in 1948. He then won from Congress a few welfare programs including expanded Social Security payments, an increased minimum wage, and enlarged federal support for housing. Emphasis on national security, however, overshadowed these gains. Indeed, Truman's remarkable election occurred during the Berlin crisis. The following year the United States established the North Atlantic Treaty Organization to check Soviet expansion in western Europe. America's nuclear monopoly ended when the Soviets successfully detonated their first atomic device; in addition, Mao Tse-tung defeated the Nationalists under Chiang Kai-shek, establishing China as the most populous communist nation in the world. During the summer of 1950 communist North Korea invaded the pro-western South, while other communist and nationalist groups struggled against the French in Southeast Asia.

Black perceived how these national security threats came to be translated into threats against domestic freedom. After Truman's reelection, the House Committee on Un-American Activities and a counterpart Senate committee dominated by the Republican Senator from Wisconsin, Joseph McCarthy, increasingly exploited the growing fear of communism. The President implemented a federal loyalty program, which made government employment dependent upon taking an oath denying association with communist beliefs or organizations. The measure heightened the nationwide fear of communist conspiracy. Yet much of the difficulty arose from the problem of distinguishing between guilt by association and conspiracy. Truman's loyalty program aimed not simply at free speech but at conspiracy. Truman's program recognized the distinction. McCarthy did not and therefore caused harm to many innocent people by fostering guilt by association. Meanwhile, liberals obscured the issue, insisting that it was all merely a witch hunt. Moreover, some of the investigations by the House and Senate committees used tactics Black himself had used in the 1930s, though he may well not have seen the connection.

These tensions reached inside the Court. The congressional investigation and subsequent conviction for perjury of Alger Hiss focused public attention on Frankfurter, who appeared in court as a character witness on behalf of the former State Department official. About the same time, Julius and Ethel Rosenberg were convicted for providing the Soviets with secret information that facilitated development of the atom bomb. Douglas and Black were publicly identified with the controversial attempt to have the Court review the Rosenbergs' case. In addition, Black feared a still greater threat to individual rights when Congress, over Truman's veto, passed the McCarran Internal Security Act of 1950. Although the measure did not outlaw the Communist party, it required certain organizations designated as security risks to register with the government and to publish their internal records.

The Black family suffered indirectly from this uproar. Virginia and Clifford Durr, Josephine's sister and brother-in-law, were often attacked because as a lawyer Clifford represented clients challenging the loyalty oaths or appearing before congressional inquiries. Durr was an administrator for the Federal Communications Commission until he resigned in protest over Truman's loyalty oath program. He was also involved in the

National Lawyers' Guild, an organization known for its defense of communists. In addition, Virginia was a candidate for the U.S. Senate on the Progressive party ticket in 1948.

Josephine gave her relatives moral support, which became increasingly vital when their troubles mounted, climaxing in 1951 when Clifford was forced to resign from his position as an attorney for a labor union. Josephine's intense emotional involvement created a traumatic struggle for inner peace that she strove to overcome by studying Christian Science. Nevertheless, on December 7, 1951, at age fifty-one, she suffered a heart attack in her sleep and died.

Josephine's death devastated the Justice. When Hugo, Jr., arrived at the family home, he found Black behind his desk looking like "nothing I'd ever seen before. He just sat staring straight ahead, tears shining on his face, his teeth grinding together." After Josephine's funeral in Arlington National Cemetery, Black emerged from the "trance-like state of depression." Yet the pain did not abate. Perhaps he had not done enough, perhaps he should have resigned from the Court when Josephine so often struggled with illness. As a practicing lawyer, he would have had more money to provide even better medical care.

The Blacks' children were entering new phases of life that brought closer the tensions of public affairs. Daughter Josephine graduated from high school and started at Swarthmore. Hugo and Sterling completed their educations, Hugo graduating from law school at Yale and Sterling at Columbia. Both married, and each began practicing law, Hugo in Birmingham and Sterling in Los Alamos, New Mexico. Black counseled them with fatherly love and wisdom, providing numerous references to the works of historians such as Willard Hurst and Joseph Dorfman, and classical writers such as Tacitus and Cicero. At one point he underlined a passage from Tacitus revealing that a climate of fear and despair was not new under the sun. Never, Tacitus had written, was the community "in a state of deeper anxiety and alarm, never was there greater need of caution against a man's nearest relatives; men were afraid to meet, afraid to discourse:

silence and distrust extended alike to strangers and acquaintances, and both were equally avoided: Even things dumb and inanimate, roofs and walls, were regarded with apprehension."

Other close associations heightened Black's sensitivity to the threat of McCarthyism. Florida Senator Claude Pepper, Black's distant relative and old friend with whom he had served briefly before joining the Court, having earned the title of "red pepper," was defeated for reelection in 1950. Black's son Hugo, a partner with Jerome Cooper in a firm representing various unions, worked under pressure from popular fear that organized labor was affiliated with communism.

Conflict also arose over the Truman Administration's call for civil rights legislation. In the summer of 1950 Black doubted that it would be wise for him to visit Alabama because of high emotions over the segregation cases.

Postwar liberalism was in crisis. Roosevelt's death removed the individual personality and symbol that had provided continuity to national policymaking since 1933; and the conservative coalition in Congress and national security concerns impeded Truman's revival of social welfare policies, developments that did not in themselves ensure the demise of New Deal liberalism. In *Korematsu* and other decisions Black had countenanced the restriction of individual rights out of an overriding belief that his nation's enemies threatened American democracy and the Constitution. Now, however, an unexpected challenge had emerged. The anguish caused his family and friends, who he knew were loyal Americans, reinforced his conviction that the postwar subordination of individual rights to majoritarian democracy was unwarranted. Furthermore, Black was convinced that leaders such as McCarthy were exploiting the public's fear of communist subversion solely to increase their own power.

The Court's membership changed. In September 1945, to succeed Roberts, Truman appointed the Republican senator from Ohio, Harold H. Burton. The following spring, Stone collapsed while reading an opinion from the bench and died. Black then became the Court's senior member and, according to custom, he took over the duties of chief justice until Truman appointed the wartime administrator and former federal judge, Democrat Frederick M. Vinson of Kentucky, as Stone's successor. In 1949 Rutledge and Murphy died, and their successors were Truman's attorney general, Tom C. Clark of Texas, and Black's old friend, the Democratic senator from Indiana, Sherman Minton.

Conflict within the Court became public. When Stone died and Black took over temporarily as chief justice, Jackson made a bitter public statement from Nuremberg disclaiming any interest in the position of chief justice. Furthermore, he revealed the Jewell Ridge controversy, in which Black had refused to withdraw from the cases in which his former law partner represented one of the litigants. Jackson's revelation was motivated by Frankfurter's intimation (not based on fact) that Black was lobbying to become chief justice. As the clash made the headlines, Truman exclaimed that the "Supreme Court has really made a mess of itself." He then nominated Vinson, a loyal friend and capable politician, who possessed an "uncanny knack of placating opposing minds."

More profound divisions had meanwhile developed, especially over cases involving individual rights and governmental power. Immediately following the Japanese attack on Pearl Harbor the governor of Hawaii had proclaimed martial law, suspended the writ of habeas corpus, and delegated administrative responsibilities to the military authorities. The area's military commander then closed the civil courts, established military tribunals to try civilians without juries, and denied any right of appeal to federal courts. Reviewing the laws governing civil justice in Hawaii and the history of martial law, Black held the military's actions unlawful in *Duncan* v. *Kahanamoku* (1946). Frankfurter and Burton dissented on the ground that wartime necessity warranted military control. Black in a letter to Stone conceded that the President's wartime powers were vital to preserving "public safety" in combat zones. All evidence demonstrated, however, that Hawaii was not threatened with direct involvement in battle. The military had established, contrary to the *Milligan* precedent, which had been central to the German saboteurs case, a "totalitarian program" on the basis of a "wartime necessity" that did not exist.

Also in 1946 the Court without dissent upheld the rights of suspected communists against congressional harassment. During the war, Congress had prohibited the payment of salaries to thirty-nine federal employees attacked as "crackpot, radical bureaucrats" and affiliates of "communist front organizations." Robert M. Lovett and others sued for recovery in the Court of Claims, which decided in their favor. The federal government then appealed to the Supreme Court in *U.S.* v. *Lovett,* and Black wrote the opinion. "What is involved here," he said, "is a congressional proscription of Lovett" and others, "prohibiting their ever holding a government job." Black saw this as a bill of attainder, defined in the late-nineteenth-century Reconstruction era decisions as an unconstitutional "legislative act which inflicts punishment without judicial trial." Black did not address the question whether anyone had a right to a government job, or whether being deprived of such a job could properly be called "attainder."

Black was less concerned about the rights of America's wartime enemies. He concurred in the decision of the *Yamashita* case (1946) upholding a special military tribunal that had tried, convicted, and ordered the execution of a commanding general of the Imperial Japanese Army for violating the laws of war, thus rejecting the dissenting views of Murphy and Rutledge that the trial violated the due process guarantees of the Fifth Amendment. A year later Black again joined the majority in *Haupt* v. *U.S.,* upholding the treason conviction and life-imprisonment sentence of Max Haupt. Haupt's son had been one of the saboteurs, and the father had sheltered young Haupt, helped him to buy a car, and assisted him to obtain employment in a defense plant. These "overt acts" warranted the charge of treason. Murphy dissented, however, arguing for the application of the more libertarian standard governing treason that had been established during the war.

Black was again at odds with his more libertarian colleagues in *Knauer* v. *U.S.* (1946). The Court upheld the removal of citizenship from a "thoroughgoing Nazi and a faithful follower of Adolf Hitler," who had become a naturalized U.S. citizen for the express purpose of furthering the German cause before the war. Murphy and Rutledge dissented because they felt that the government's action threatened the broader rights of citizenship. In a brief concurrence Black explained that Knauer's own statements during a "fair trial" left no doubt that despite his oath to the contrary he had continued to serve Germany "with the same fanatical zeal which motivated the saboteurs sent to the United States to wage war."

These decisions suggested Black's view regarding civil liberties at the start of the Cold War. In cases involving the rights of those directly or indirectly affiliated with the nation's enemies, he deferred to government authority. During wartime the Constitution permitted a broad subordination of individual rights to congressional and executive power. In addition, since a declaration of war had determined that national survival was threatened, community interest should prevail over individual liberty. After the war, however, these same concerns of national welfare demanded, as the *Kahanamoku* decision showed, the firmest possible protection for the rights of American citizens.

Fears concerning national security and communist subversion, however, put Black on the defensive. The case of *American Communications Association* v. *Douds* (1950) arose out of the union's refusal to comply with the anticommunist oath provisions of the Taft-Hartley Act. The union argued that the oath violated the freedom of speech and conscience guaranteed by the First Amendment. The federal government claimed that the law's requirements represented a valid exercise of the commerce power, which was the constitutional basis of the Taft-Hartley Act. Chief Justice Vinson sustained the law. In dissent, Black said Vinson's decision undermined the "freedom to think" as an "absolute" right. "Centuries of experience testify that laws aimed at one political or religious group" generated "hatreds and prejudices which rapidly spread beyond control." He recognized that, like anyone else, communists committing "overt acts" in violation of valid laws could be punished. This did not, however, justify assigning "guilt" by "association or affiliation." The foundation of the First Amendment was, Black stressed, that "our free institutions can be maintained without proscribing or penalizing political belief, speech, press assembly, or party affiliation."

The next year another significant test of Black's stand on individual liberty occurred in *Dennis* v. *U.S.* During Truman's reelection campaign the Justice Department had initiated prosecutions of Eugene Dennis and other top American Communist Party leaders under the Smith Act of 1940, which made illegal the advocacy of the overthrow of the United States, and forbade conspiracy to commit such action or membership in any group supporting such action. In spectacular trials during 1949, the government charged that the philosophical underpinnings of the Communist Party violated the "advocacy" and "conspiracy" provisions of the law. Following the federal district judge's instructions construing those words broadly, the jury decided against Dennis and the others. On appeal Vinson's majority opinion held that it was not necessary to "wait until the putsch is about to be executed, the plans have been laid, and the signal is awaited." The government could define the risk of clear and present danger in terms of whether "the gravity of the evil, discounted by its improbability, justifies such invasion of free speech as is necessary to avoid the danger."

Only Black and Douglas dissented. Although they disagreed with the tenets of the Communist Party, they opposed prosecution in the absence of overt acts. Douglas noted that the whereabouts and daily action of Dennis and virtually every party member were known to the F.B.I. Arrest was virtually inevitable, therefore, should communism create any threat to national security. Black emphasized that the real motive behind the trials was that the American communist leaders "agreed to assemble and to talk and publish certain ideas." Vinson's opinion was a "virulent form of prior censorship" which "waters down the First Amendment so that it amounts to little more than an admonition to Congress," securing only those "safe or orthodox views" rarely needing protection. Black hoped that in "calmer times, when present pressures, passions and fears subside, this or some later Court will restore the First Amendment liberties to the high preferred place where they belong in a free society."

For Black the *Douds* and *Dennis* decisions revealed the consequences of the nation's preoccupation with communist subversion. Black conceded that most Americans probably shared the view expressed in a letter which he received in April 1950, from someone he had never met: The "Communist Party is more than a political party. It is an organ of Stalin's conspiracy to conquer the world." The experience of his family members and friends demonstrated how such fears created guilt by association, undermining the individual freedom upon which community welfare depended. Thus, although a majority of the Court sought to safeguard Americans by deferring to the government's suppression of unpopular beliefs, Black and Douglas sought to protect constitutional liberty by distinguishing the advocacy of controversial doctrines from overt conduct. The best way to defend American democracy was by allowing communists to compete in the marketplace of ideas.

Finally, Black was able to establish a significant limitation on expanding presidential power. The Korean hostilities made a continuous supply of steel vital to the military effort. During the winter and spring of 1952 the Truman Administration supported contract negotiations between the steel industry and the United Steel Workers in order to avoid a strike. When the effort failed, the union set April 9 as the beginning of a nationwide walkout. Truman responded by an executive order authorizing his secretary of commerce, Charles Sawyer, to seize and operate the steel mills in the name of the government. Although the President invited congressional action, he based his order on implied executive powers of the sort Black had affirmed in *Saboteur* and *Korematsu*. Truman did so because no act of Congress permitted the government to take over private property in order to settle a labor dispute in peacetime. He declined to use the procedure of the Taft-Hartley Act authorizing an eighty-day postponement.

Roosevelt had seized private property during World War II, and Black had supported such actions for the very reason that Congress *had* declared war. Wilson and Lincoln had committed similar wartime acts, again with congressional approval. That was not the case during the Korean conflict. The steel companies noted the lack of a formal congressional declaration of war and asked for an injunction from the federal district court to stop the President. Given the nation's preoccupation with security and the concomitant expansion of peacetime executive authority, Truman believed that he was justified even after the lower court granted the companies' request. The government appealed until the case reached the Supreme Court in *Youngstown Sheet and Tube Co.* v. *Sawyer* (1952).

Black wrote the leading opinion affirming the power of the lower court to issue the injunction. He conceded that in time of war the executive's authority was greater than in time of peace. The Constitution conferred upon Congress, however, the duty to declare war, and until Congress did so, no necessity justified a president's seizure of private property. Moreover, Black repeatedly stressed that if a threat to national security existed, Congress had provided Truman the means to meet it through the Taft-Hartley Act. Assertion of implied executive prerogatives did not obscure the fact that the President had ignored the will of Congress. "The Founders of this Nation entrusted the lawmaking power to the Congress alone in both good and bad times," Black said. "The fears of power and the hopes for freedom that lay behind their choice . . . would confirm our holding that this seizure order cannot stand."

Although five justices wrote concurring opinions agreeing that Truman had exceeded his powers in this particular instance, only Douglas accepted Black's strict interpretation of separation of powers. The other four justices saw the line between congressional and executive authority as more ambiguous, suggesting that given different facts they might have upheld the President. Chief Justice Vinson, joined by Reed and

Minton, dissented, arguing that the President possessed broad discretionary prerogatives. "Those who suggest that this is a case involving extraordinary powers should be mindful that these are extraordinary times," Vinson said. Truman's own advisers undermined this view, however, by admitting that the American public had "never believed" the President's claim of the need for "uninterrupted steel production," and in the "face of recent releases of steel for race tracks and bowling alleys, they are even less likely to believe this now."

Black faced further difficulties in cases involving the status of individual rights in the states. In *Colegrove* v. *Green* (1946) the issue was whether legislative malapportionment violated the equal protection clause of the Fourteenth Amendment. Because the population of rural as compared to urban voting districts had declined since the late nineteenth century, urban areas were significantly under-represented in Congress and in the state legislatures. Nevertheless, in a 4–to–3 majority Frankfurter joined his three colleagues in holding that the Court should exercise restraint and not enter the "political thicket." Black, however, led the dissenters in stating: "What is involved here is the right to vote guaranteed by the Federal Constitution. It has always been the rule that where a federally protected right has been invaded the federal courts will provide the remedy to rectify the wrong done."

Black also had problems regarding the relationship between the First and the Fourteenth amendments. After the dramatic turnabout in the second flag-salute case of 1943, Black and the majority had used the due process clause to restrict the states' authority. By 1949, however, Black's activism increasingly gave way to Frankfurter's restraint. In *Feiner* v. *New York* (1951) a Jewish student on a street corner used a loudspeaker to criticize Truman and other public figures and to suggest that blacks should rise and claim individual rights. After threatening remarks from a crowd, the police asked Feiner to stop. When he resisted, he was arrested and convicted of disorderly conduct. A 5–to–4 majority upheld the conviction, but Black dissented. The police should have defended Feiner's right to speak, he said; they should not have bowed to popular animosity.

Black's absolute defense of free speech was tested on the issue of picketing. Black noted that unlike spoken or written expression, which was given constitutional preference, peaceful picketing was a form of conduct that acquired First Amendment protection only in cases where its use closely approximated traditional speech.

Other First Amendment challenges involved the establishment of religion clause. Thomas Jefferson had set forth the position that a "wall of separation" existed between church and state, including the prohibition of tax support for religious instruction. *Everson* v. *Board of Education* (1947) concerned a New Jersey law authorizing local school boards to reimburse parents for bus fares their children paid to attend either public or Catholic schools. A local taxpayer charged that the school board's plan violated the establishment clause. After winning in a lower court, the taxpayer lost on review by the state's highest tribunal, whereupon he appealed to the Supreme Court.

Black wrote the majority opinion. The issue was, he said, whether the state could provide this particular public service without violating the First Amendment's establishment clause. He equated the expenditure of tax dollars to ensure children's safe transport to both public and Catholic schools with the use of such funds to support police protection for all children. Black reviewed the history of the nation's experience with religious establishment, concluding that the First Amendment required the "state to be a neutral in its relations with groups of religious believers and unbelievers." In this case the state neither contributed money nor otherwise supported the parochial schools. It merely provided a "general program to help parents get their children, regardless of their religion, safely and expeditiously to and from accredited schools." Finally, Black affirmed, the wall separating church and state "must be kept high and impregnable. We could not approve the slightest breach. New Jersey has not breached it here."

In *Everson,* Frankfurter and two other justices joined Jackson in dissenting. The "undertones of the opinion, advocating complete and uncompromising separation of Church from State," Jackson said, "seem utterly discordant with its conclusion yielding support to their commingling in educational matters." Others shared this view. A Methodist pastor informed the Justice that his decision was "most unwise for our democracy if not down right shortsighted and stupid." An anonymous critic wrote Black that the decision resulted from a conspiracy to clear the Justice's "skirts of the charges in the Ku Klux Klan matter," in order to favor "corporations, unions, communists," and the "Catholic Hierarchy, which behind the scenes" ruled "some of our big cities and controls the greatest patronage office of both parties."

The critics underestimated Black's attempt to articulate principles governing the establishment of religion. Black was no more willing than Jackson to breach the wall separating church and state. At the same time he was certain that establishing the principle of governmental neutrality where safety was at stake successfully preserved the inviolability of the establishment clause. After all, New Jersey's legislature had conferred the reimbursement authority upon local school officials to assist without preference both the public school majority and the Catholic school minority.

The limits of Black's neutrality principle became more apparent the next year in *McCollum* v. *Board of Education.* A state law permitted religious instruction within school buildings during regular school hours. Under a "released time arrangement" pupils whose parents signed "request cards" attended classes taught by outside teachers representing various religious faiths. Black's opinion for the Court held that "beyond all question" the policy violated the establishment clause as interpreted in the *Everson* decision. Yet in *Zorach* v. *Clauson* (1952) the Court sustained a New York law permitting released time from public school for religious instruction since that instruction was carried on in separate buildings not supported by tax funds. Black dissented, arguing that it was only "by wholly isolating the state from the religious sphere and compelling it to be completely neutral, that the freedom of each and every denomination and of all non-believers can be maintained."

Black's search for rules to govern the application of the First Amendment to the states was part of a larger conflict. Frankfurter's commitment to judicial restraint underlaid his position that the liberties applicable to the states through the due process clause were merely *similar* to those in the Bill of Rights. As a result, the judge was free to prefer the interest of the majority over that of the individual. Black countered, however, that the rights found in the due process clause and the first eight amendments were *identical*. Accordingly, judges were bound to protect individual liberty to a degree neither more nor less than that specifically required by the Bill of Rights. He believed that total incorporation limited judicial discretion and increased individual freedom. The theory of incorporation frightened Frankfurter and others because, in effect, due process under the Fourteenth Amendment could stretch almost indefinitely. But Black countered that a strict regard for the Bill of Rights, read literally, restricted the judge.

Black pronounced his theory of incorporation in his dissenting opinion in *Adamson* v. *California* (1948). The case raised the question whether evidence used in a state trial resulting in a murder conviction was admissible in light of the Fifth Amendment's privilege against self-incrimination. The Court held that the Amendment did not apply to the state under the due process clause. Black argued to the contrary that the entire Bill of Rights restricted the states. "I would follow what I believe was the original purpose of the Fourteenth Amendment," he said, "to extend to all the people of the nation the complete protection of the Bill of Rights. To hold that this Court can determine what, if any, provisions of the Bill of Rights will be enforced, and if so to what degree, is to frustrate the great design of a written Constitution."

The Court's response to Black's theory was mixed. In *Wolf* v. *Colorado* (1949) Frankfurter's opinion held that, although the Fourth Amendment itself was not part of the due process clause, the basic guarantee against arbitrary search and seizure by the authorities did apply to the states. The Court went further in *Rochin* v. *California* (1952), declaring that the use of a stomach pump to obtain evidence, though medically supervised, was so shocking that it violated the due process clause. In both cases Black concurred on the basis of the theory of total incorporation, but he objected to relying on the Fourth Amendment because its phraseology of "unreasonableness" was too vague to guide authorities. The tension between the two Justices' views obscured the degree to which Black defended individual rights primarily as a means of saving democracy from itself.

Ironically, the same Cold War strains that threatened some civil liberties fostered the erosion of racial segregation. The NAACP initiated more suits after 1945 than ever before. Truman's Justice Department joined some of the cases. In *Shelley* v. *Kraemer* (1948) Black and a unanimous Court overturned restrictive covenants in private agreements that forbade the sale of property to racial and ethnic minorities as a violation of the equal protection clause of the Fourteenth Amendment. The government's justification for supporting civil rights in this case was that the "United States has been embarrassed in the conduct of foreign relations by acts of discrimination taking place in this country."

Black revealed his concern about the implications of American racism in decisions that overturned the California restrictions on property rights of Japanese-Americans. When Murphy used sweeping rhetoric to condemn such "out right racial discrimination," Black suggested that "softer blows" would serve just as well while not doing "us harm" abroad. Black noted that a similar argument emerged from the politically controversial report of the President's newly established Committee on Civil Rights, which in turn influenced the Justice Department's stand against segregated railroad dining car service in the South, a position the Court upheld in *Henderson* v. *U.S.* (1950).

The Court now faced a turning point on racial segregation. As Black and the three other Southern justices knew firsthand, the region's refusal to support equal public education fundamentally undermined the social welfare, economic opportunity, and self-respect of black Americans. The Court's separate-but-equal doctrine established in *Plessy* v. *Ferguson* (1896) provided the constitutional foundation for racial discrimination in public education as well as in other areas of life. Black was still a new justice in 1938 when the Court interpreted the *Plessy* doctrine to hold for the first time that Missouri had unconstitutionally excluded blacks from its law school. Not until a decade later, however, did the Court require the admission of a black woman, Ada Lois Sipuel, to the public law school of Oklahoma, holding her exclusion solely for reasons of race was not consistent with the rule in *Plessy*.

The Court divided two years later when the NAACP appealed two new suits. *McLaurin* v. *Oklahoma* involved racial segregation in the state's graduate education programs, whereas *Sweatt* v. *Painter* concerned a Texas state law school. Both cases urged that the Court overrule *Plessy*. A profound split developed. Vinson leaned toward upholding Texas but not Oklahoma, while avoiding any direct question of *Plessy*. Douglas rejected doing either. Black favored holding against the states on the ground that segregation in graduate education was improper, yet he did not consider that the time was ripe to overturn outright the separate-but-equal doctrine. Gradually, the Court agreed on a compromise consistent with Black's position. The Court decided unanimously that racially segregated graduate education violated the equal protection clause of the Fourteenth Amendment. There was, however, no mention of overruling the *Plessy* doctrine.

For Black the segregation cases were part of a broader set of strains within liberalism. Political exigencies arising from international pressures encouraged the conservative coalition in Congress and the President to meet the threat of communist subversion with the full power of government. Black urged a restriction on the President's peacetime emergency prerogatives, the establishment of a rigid separation between congressional and executive powers, and the application of the Bill of Rights as an absolute guarantee against government interference. However, by 1952 it was often only as a dissenter that Black was able to argue for more rather than less individual freedom to save American liberalism. Nonetheless, in the wartime enemies cases, Murphy and Rutledge argued for expanded civil liberties; Black viewed individual rights and community welfare as interdependent. By assaulting individual freedom in order to protect democracy, McCarthyism actually undermined the rights upon which democracy depended. Black's faith in unchanging human nature convinced him that the best means of ameliorating fear was greater liberty guaranteed by clear consitutional prescriptions. As Truman's presidency ended, Black saw hope for the revitalization of liberalism in the NAACP's struggle for civil rights.

CHAPTER EIGHT

Uncertain Revolution (1952–1960)

❖
❖

After 1952 Black contributed significantly to the most revolutionary civil rights decisions in the Court's history. Meanwhile, although the Court increasingly upheld results consistent with Black's defense of the Bill of Rights, it rejected the constitutional principles he developed to reach those results. This conflict reflected the nation's ambiguous acceptance of big government and liberalism itself.

Black undoubtedly viewed the closing months of the Truman administration with ambivalence. His *Youngstown* opinion was a stinging rebuke to the President who had struggled to maintain liberalism. Black was hardly gratified when Senator Pat McCarran, a leading proponent of McCarthyism, praised the decision of "our former colleague" from Alabama. Indeed, Black was concerned enough about the President's being "so upset" that he gave a party at his home for him and the members of the Court. "We all went and poured a lot of bourbon down Harry Truman," Douglas observed. "He didn't change his mind, but he felt better at least for a few hours." Soon thereafter, the Democrats' twenty-year control of the presidency ended with the election of Dwight D. Eisenhower.

In addition, conflict arising from the Court's desegregation decisions of 1950 increased. Black was concerned but not surprised when his former Senate and judicial colleague, South Carolina governor James F. Byrnes, criticized the erosion of segregation. According to one North Carolina newspaper, Black noted, Byrnes "declared that if the United States Supreme Court should order abandonment of segregation in the public schools" South Carolina would "abolish its public schools."

Under Vinson the Court had restricted the Fourteenth Amendment's *Plessy* doctrine in order to invalidate segregation in graduate schools. Encouraged by these decisions, the NAACP attacked racial discrimination in grade schools. Seeking to demonstrate the broad-based character of racial injustice, the NAACP initiated suits simultaneously in South Carolina, Virginia, Delaware, Kansas, and Washington, D.C., arguing that segregation, and therefore *Plessy,* was wrong. The cases reached the Supreme Court in December 1952. The Court consolidated the four state suits under the style of the Kansas litigation, *Brown* v. *Board of Education,* while treating separately the federal questions raised in the Washington appeal, *Bolling* v. *Sharpe.*

Brown "severely divided" the justices. Black, Douglas, and perhaps two or three others wanted to overrule *Plessy* outright, whereas Vinson, Frankfurter, and probably Reed and Jackson hesitated to go that far. Vinson argued that reversing *Plessy* altogether, rather than merely restricting its application as the Court had done in the graduate-education decisions, would mean "complete abolition of public schools in some areas." Moreoever, even those agreeing with Black could not suggest how the Court might implement a decision ending a social and legal practice of over fifty years. The wrangling was intractable enough that during June 1953, the Court ordered the parties to file supplemental briefs and postponed further arguments until October.

Before the Court reconsidered the five suits it declined to agree with Black's opinion in *Terry* v. *Adams* (1953). In 1944 the Court had declared that the southern states' all-white primary elections violated the Fifteenth Amendment. The *Terry* case involved a Texas county's selection of candidates through a private club known as the Jaybirds, which explicitly excluded blacks. Black held that even though the procedure was carried on by a private group, its operation was so intimately involved in the public process of choosing candidates that it was invalid under the Fifteenth Amendment. Although eight of the nine justices accepted the result, two separate concurring opinions and a dissent challenged Black's reasoning. Moreover, the justices disagreed on what standards should govern the implementation of the *Jaybird* decision.

Then on September 8, 1953, four weeks before the scheduled reargument of the desegregation suits, Chief Justice Vinson died. The Senate expeditiously confirmed as his successor California governor Earl Warren, whereupon the Court again postponed reargument of *Brown* and *Bolling* until early December so that Warren could study the cases. Warren knew that any decision would be controversial, not only because of the emotions associated with racial justice itself but also because of the South's clout in national politics. Black admitted, moreover, that overruling *Plessy* would mean the "end of political liberalism in the South" and bring extremists "out of the woodwork." The Klan would "ride again." However, racial segregation gave the Soviet Union a powerful Cold War propaganda weapon.

As a result, the Court considered carefully the Eisenhower administration's response to *Brown* and *Bolling*. The lame-duck Truman Justice Department had filed a brief supporting the desegregation of public schools. Eisenhower allowed his Justice Department to file briefs consistent with the position of its Democratic predecessor. The administration's action helped to ameliorate the Court's divisiveness by the time Vinson died. During the rearguments of *Brown* the members of the Court gave Thurgood Marshall, the NAACP's chief council, little difficulty. Instead, they repeatedly asked the administration's Solicitor General, J. Lee Rankin, what sort of standards might govern enforcement of desegregation if *Plessy* was overruled. Rankin suggested that the rules controlling implementation "might involve the principle of handling the matter with deliberate speed."

After the December arguments it was apparent that a growing majority agreed that separate was *not* equal. Black and Frankfurter had consistently insisted on the importance of unanimous decisions in segregation cases in order to establish public support for the Court. As a result, early in 1954 Warren sought to reach unanimity in *Brown*. After considerable study the justices concluded that the intent of the Fourteenth Amendment's framers was too ambiguous to provide sufficient justification for consensus. Meanwhile, the NAACP influenced the Court's opinion by presenting social science data that suggested racial discrimination in public education hurt black children's self-respect. The evidence was of particular interest to Black, whose success as a lawyer and public official had been due in large part to his keen appreciation of the importance of respectability to individual and community welfare. In addition Warren appealed to his colleagues' judgment by emphasizing that the Court's precedents since World War II pointed toward ending segregation.

Above all, however, the chief justice stressed that the Court should postpone determination of the standard governing implementation of desegregation. With Frankfurter's help, he convinced the justices that a unanimous decision overruling *Plessy* would facilitate the formulation of an enforcement decree later on.

By May 17, 1954, Warren achieved the unanimity that Black and Frankfurter had considered essential. In *Brown* he held for all the justices that "in the field of public education the doctrine of 'separate but equal' has no place. Separate educational facilities are inherently unequal." As a result, the black children in the four suits consolidated in the *Brown* case, "by reason of the segregation complained of," had been "deprived of the equal protection of the laws guaranteed by the Fourteenth Amendment." While Warren referred to the NAACP's social science data as significant evidence, he relied primarily on the graduate-education decisions of 1950 as precedent. He called on the southern states, the Justice Department, and the NAACP to file briefs regarding appropriate standards the Court should follow in an enforcement decree.

On the same day, in *Bolling* v. *Sharp* Warren declared that racial segregation in Washington's public schools was unconstitutional. He followed Black's and Frankfurter's idea of reading into the due process clause of the Fifth Amendment the constitutional principle of equal protection. Such judicial activism, according to Black, was justified by his theory of incorporation. Warren's *Bolling* opinion, he said, "merely recognized what had been the understanding from the beginning of the country, an understanding shared by many of the draftsmen of the Fourteenth Amendment, that the whole Bill of Rights, including the Due Process Clause of the Fifth Amendment, was a guarantee that all persons would receive equal treatment under the law."

As the Court heard arguments concerning the implementation decree in *Brown,* public pressure mounted. Opposition to the decision was so intense in the Deep South that Alabama, Georgia, Louisiana, and Mississippi refused to submit briefs. The southern states that did comply merely urged delay. Black conveyed his awareness of such emotion in a letter to Hugo, Jr. "I think you are correct in believing that this might not be the most pleasant time for me to visit Birmingham," he wrote. Perhaps the saddest comment was the refusal of Black's law school graduation class to invite him to its fiftieth anniversary reunion.

Eisenhower explicitly refused to support *Brown.* Instead, the President stated repeatedly that he did not believe "you can change the hearts of men with laws or decisions." He did, however, order the expeditious enforcement of *Bolling* v. *Sharp* in Washington's public schools. Eisenhower also stood firm when southern Democrats attempted to prevent confirmation of John Marshall Harlan as associate justice of the Supreme Court because of his support of civil rights. The President appointed the Republican Harlan from the federal appellate bench after Justice Jackson died in October 1954.

In April 1955, the Court finally discussed in conference the decree implementing the *Brown* decision. Although the justices disagreed on substantive details, a majority shared Black's views. He believed that "the less we say, the better off we are," since the South would accept desegregation with extreme reluctance. He also supported the need for unanimity in any decision. Finally, he emphasized, "nothing" was "more important than that this Court should not issue what it cannot enforce."

Frankfurter's role was also vital. He had helped to bring about unanimity by contending that the principle that should ultimately guide the implementation decree was one that the

Solicitor General had articulated as early as 1952, encapsulated in the phrase "with all deliberate speed." The other members of the Court probably never knew that the ambiguous phase found its way into the government's brief because Frankfurter had given it to Philip Elman, a Justice Department attorney and one of Frankfurter's former law clerks. The "trick" was to formulate "criteria not too loose to invite evasion yet with enough give to leave room for variant problems." Although some justices wanted to fix a specific date for the completion of desegregation, Frankfurter argued that such action would "tend to alienate instead of enlist favorable or educable local sentiment."

The views of Black and Frankfurter influenced Warren's second *Brown* decision (*Brown* II), announced on May 31, 1955. The Court left the responsibility for implementing the "constitutional principles" of *Brown* to the federal district judges, who were expected to approach the "varied local problems" with "practical flexibility." During the transition to desegregated schools "it should go without saying that the vitality of these constitutional principles cannot be allowed to yield simply because of disagreement with them." Meanwhile, although school authorities were required to make a "prompt and reasonable start" toward compliance, what these words meant was to be decided by the district judges. Desegregation was to occur at the "earliest practicable date," with delay permissible where problems of "administration" arose. Finally, the character of Warren's short decision was distilled in a closing phrase. The four cases combined under the *Brown* style were returned to the lower courts to initiate decrees that would open public schools to black students "on a racially nondiscriminatory basis with all deliberate speed."

The ambiguity inherent in the concept of "deliberate speed" encouraged resistance. In Washington, Baltimore, and a few cities of the upper South, local officials began almost immediately to plan for desegregation. Throughout most of the Old Confederacy, however, the response ranged from doing nothing to outright defiance. Within a year after the *Brown* II decision most southern United States congressmen and senators signed the Southern Manifesto, pledging "to use all lawful means to bring about a reversal of this decision which is contrary to the Constitution and to prevent the use of force in its implementation." A majority of southern legislatures passed resolutions of interposition, drawing upon state-sovereignty ideas to nullify *Brown*. Many leading southern politicians promised to abolish public schools rather than permit intermingling and "race mongrelization." The South's massive resistance revealed that a significant confrontation was unavoidable.

Eisenhower's response to *Brown* II was not encouraging. The federal government's brief presented during April declared that the "responsibility for achieving compliance with the Court's decision" did not "rest on the judiciary alone. Every officer and agency of government, federal, state, and local, is likewise charged with the duty of enforcing the Constitution and the rights guaranteed under it." To Black's dismay, however, when local officials in Texas and Tennessee blocked desegregation the federal government refused to intervene.

Moreover, Black witnessed firsthand the difficulties federal district courts faced. Early in 1956 university authorities and a white mob forced the withdrawal and ultimate expulsion of Autherine Lucy, the first black student admitted to the University of Alabama. Justice Black was involved tangentially in a unsuccessful appeal of the Alabama federal court's decision upholding the public officials' actions. A more favorable result might have resulted had the federal government supported the appeal. Indeed, in Hoxie, Arkansas, in the one instance during this period where the Justice Department intervened to help enforce a federal court order, desegregation prevailed despite vigorous opposition.

Still, in other areas the nation retained and even broadened the benefits of New Deal liberalism. A federal government controlled by Republicans extended the Social Security system to include another 10 million people and unemployment compensation to 4 million more. It increased the minimum wage and federal aid to education and housing. These policies applied to all Americans without regard to race.

At the same time, the Republican administration made moderate progress on overcoming racial discrimination in other areas. During 1955–56, it enforced the ICC's ban on segregated public accommodations in interstate travel. Federal authorities sustained the Court's desegregation of public buses, fostered by the boycott led by young Martin Luther King, Jr., in Montgomery, Alabama. Moreover, enactment of the Civil Rights Act of 1957 strengthened judicial enforcement of voting rights in the South.

Yet, Black could not help noting, Eisenhower's moderation reflected the liberal dilemma. The President's expansion of big government, like Roosevelt's New Deal, improved the welfare and opportunity of white as well as black Americans. Southerners, moreover, acquiesced in the comparative economic improvement of blacks so long as it did not fundamentally threaten white supremacy. During the 1950s the Eisenhower administration wanted to win over to the Republican party black voters in the urban North, but it also sought to exploit southern fears arising from Truman's support of civil rights. Thus the President compromised. Although he supported modest restriction of segregation, he discouraged vigorous federal enforcement of *Brown,* which would have struck at the heart of racial discrimination.

These exigencies gave federal judges chief responsibility for the implementation of *Brown.* When it came to elementary and secondary public education (except where federal authorities exercised full control in Washington) Eisenhower administration officials interpreted the *Brown* II standard to mean generally that the federal courts would enforce school desegregation with little help from the executive branch. As presiding justice of the Fifth U.S. Circuit Court of Appeals, including all the Deep South states from Georgia to Texas, Black was intimately aware of the consequent isolation federal judges faced.

The most significant instance of massive resistance occurred in Little Rock. During the summer of 1958 the Court held only its third special session in the twentieth century to hear *Cooper* v. *Aaron.* The case involved a school desegregation struggle begun on September 3, 1957. Governor Orval E. Faubus attracted worldwide attention. Claiming that civil disorder threatened the city, in defiance of the federal court's desegregation decree he ordered the National Guard to block the admission of nine black students to Central High School. For three weeks, Faubus, Eisenhower, the local school board, the city's black community, the NAACP, rabid segregationists, and the federal court were embroiled in intractable confrontation. When on September 20 the federal judge found the Governor's assertions concerning impending disorder groundless, Faubus complied and withdrew the Guard. But after the nine black students entered the school on September 23, a few rabble-rousers galvanized the crowd outside, forcing the students' withdrawal. The next day President Eisenhower dispatched combat-ready paratroopers, who enforced the federal court's original desegregation order.

Although troops remained at the school throughout the academic year, a coterie of segregationist-supported students harassed the black youths relentlessly. In order to end the conflict rather than defend the black students' rights, Little Rock school officials asked for and received from the federal district court a two-and-a-half-year delay in implementing desegregation. As the NAACP appealed the case of *Cooper* v. *Aaron*, Faubus began a campaign for reelection. If the Supreme Court should reverse the new court order, Faubus declared, he urged the state legislature to enact laws permitting the closure of desegregated public schools and the use of state funds to finance all-white private schools.

Little Rock was the first significant test of the enforcement of *Brown*. In a virtually unprecedented action all nine members of the Court signed the *Cooper* opinion, holding the conduct of Faubus and the state unconstitutional. The disturbances, the Court said, were "directly traceable" to the defiance of Arkansas authorities "which reflect their own determination to resist this Court's decision in the *Brown* case." Moreover, the Court asserted, the rights of black children "can neither be nullified openly and directly by state legislators or state executive or judicial officials, nor nullified indirectly by them through evasive schemes for segregation."

The Little Rock confrontation fostered rather than discouraged resistance. Even during the dramatic dispatch of paratroopers, Eisenhower did not defend the principle of the *Brown* decision. "Our personal opinions about the decision have no bearing on the matter of enforcement," the President said. This view was consistent with his insistence throughout the three weeks of confrontation that he would give Faubus "every opportunity to make an orderly retreat," so long as he complied with federal court orders. Thus, as Black noted, Eisenhower created the distinct impression that he would implement desegregation only if absolutely compelled to do so.

Black probably never knew the complete truth. In the September trial of Faubus involving his use of national guard to prevent the desegregation of Central High, the Justice Department declined to introduce evidence that demonstrated conclusively that prior to and during the crisis the Justice Department, school officials, a federal judge, and Faubus himself engaged in surreptitious contacts to end the confrontation in a manner politically advantageous to the governor. Meanwhile the Justice Department had tried, surreptitiously and unsuccessfully, to persuade the NAACP to withdraw its suit on behalf of the nine black students. Refusal to use this evidence, along with the secret negotiations, sent Faubus the clear message that the administration would enforce desegregation only in the greatest extremity.

After the Court's decision and the Governor's reelection, Faubus closed the city's high schools. Not until local white moderates cooperated with blacks in mobilizing support for a special school board election during the spring of 1959 was Faubus defeated and the schools opened to a handful of black students. The triumph, however, was of mixed value. The moderates only supported the enforcement of *Brown,* they asserted, because it was "declared law" and therefore "binding upon us. We think that the decision was erroneous and that it was a reversal of established law upon an unprecedented basis of psychology and sociology." But "we must in honesty recognize that, because the Supreme Court is the Court of last resort in the country, what it has said must stand until there is a correcting constitutional amendment or until the Court corrects its own error."

The Court's response to the Little Rock crisis also disrupted unanimity. Frankfurter and Black reached an impasse in *Cooper* v. *Aaron*. Frankfurter firmly believed that the court could foster southern popular support for *Brown* if it encouraged the region's white moderate lawyers, several of whom he had taught at Harvard. He urged the Court to make such an appeal in its *Cooper* decision. Black opposed the idea. He understood that the moderates were isolated and relatively weak. Moreover, moderates succeeded only after protracted disorder and with the assistance of the black community. Nevertheless, Frankfurter remained adamant, and a majority of the Court finally acquiesced in his writing a concurring opinion. Black was so angry with the break in unanimity that he threatened to write a dissent. However, Warren convinced him that such a course would be counterproductive.

The clash suggested the limits of judical activism on behalf of equal justice. Under Chief Justice Warren the Court reached unanimous agreement that the time had come to overturn the *Plessy* doctrine. Yet the ambiguous enforcement standard formulated in *Brown* II encouraged unanticipated defiance. As a result, Little Rock showed that except in the most extreme circumstances the Court and the federal judiciary faced massive southern resistance virtually alone.

Ironically, the Court then began shifting toward Black's views on the Bill of Rights. On June 17, 1957, the justices repudiated the restriction of civil liberties in internal security cases. In four different opinions Black voted with a new majority to invalidate government restriction of individual rights. In *Yates* v. *U.S.*, the Court overturned the conviction of several members of the Communist Party for conspiracy to advocate the overthrow of the United States. Essentially accepting Black's distinction between overt action and mere advocacy, the Court held that the communists' assertion of abstract doctrine was "too remote from concrete action to be regarded as the kind of indoctrination preparatory to action which was condemned" in the *Dennis* decision of 1951. In *Watkins* v. *U.S.* the justices reversed the conviction of a union officer for refusing to testify before the House Un-American Activities Committee concerning acquaintances in the Communist Party. In another decision, the Supreme Court reversed a New Hampshire tribunal's conviction of a university lecturer for refusing to answer questions before a state legislative investigatory committee concerning the Progressive Party. Finally, the Court struck down the discharge of a Foreign Service officer whose loyalty was improperly challenged by a federal Loyalty Review Board.

This victory of activism resulted in the "most fundamental challenge to judicial power" since Roosevelt's Court-packing plan. Indiana Senator William E. Jenner introduced a bill to limit the Court's jurisdiction. Jenner was particularly anxious about the *Watkins* decision, which he said "severely cripples, if it does not wholly smash, the Congressional power to investigate." Jenner's action was part of a broader assault on the Court led by southern opponents of *Brown* and the supporters of McCarthyism. An Alabama congressman linked *Brown*'s overturning of state-imposed racial segregation to the specter of communist subversion. Along with Warren and Douglas, Black was singled out for blame, which did not come from Southerners alone. Phoenix lawyer William H. Rehnquist denounced Black and his colleagues as "left-wingers" who made the "Constitution say what they wanted it to say." Ultimately the Jenner legislation failed in the face of opposition from the Eisenhower administration. The angry resistance fueled by *Brown* and the decisions of June 17, 1957, however, did not abate.

Consequently, by 1960 Black's increasing success in national security cases was tenuous. In *Barenblatt* v. *U.S.* (1959) the Court upheld the contempt conviction of a professor who had refused to answer questions concerning his reputed affiliation with the Communist Party. Black dissented, asserting that the majority had rejected the spirit of *Watkins* by applying a balancing test in which the government's authority triumphed over the First Amendment.

Black faced a similar challenge in other cases involving the rights of the accused under the Fourteenth Amendment. In *Griffin* v. *Illinois* (1956) the Court reviewed a state provision making the appeal of a noncapital offense contingent upon the ability to pay the costs of reproducing a trial transcript. Two indigents convicted of armed robbery, unable to pay the costs, were therefore denied appellate review. For a 5–4 majority Black held that the state's requirement violated the due process and equal protection clauses of the Fourteenth Amendment. The next year in *Breithaupt* v. *Abram,* however, the Court blunted Black's attempt to broaden the Amendment's due process guarantees. With Black in dissent, the Court held that a New Mexico conviction of an individual based on the authorities' use of a blood test, taken when he was unconscious, did not violate the due process clause.

Several factors shaped the Court's ambivalent response to Black's stand. Eisenhower appointed five members to the high bench. In addition to Warren and Harlan, he selected the Democrat, New Jersey Supreme Court judge William J. Brennan, Jr., and Republican federal judges Charles E. Whittaker and Potter Stewart to replace the retirees Minton, Reed, and Burton. Despite the turnover, however, the balance between those supporting activism or restraint remained about what it had been under Vinson. Warren and Brennan joined Black and Douglas as generally supporting the extension of individual rights. Harlan, Whittaker, and Stewart more often than not followed Frankfurter and Clark, favoring restraint.

These divisions did not prevent a gradual shift toward *results* Black considered desirable. They also encouraged, however, contrary outcomes in *Barenblatt, Griffin,* and *Breithaupt.* Although the nation's fear of communist subversion persisted, the Eisenhower administration felt secure enough to take a position against Jenner's bill, which ensured its defeat.

Even so, Black did not rely on judicial opinion alone to publicize his constitutional faith. In May 1955, he delivered a memorial address to Albert Einstein at a meeting in New York's Town Hall, which the *Times* published on its front page. The next month he was the commencement speaker at his daughter's graduation from Swarthmore College. On February 17, 1960, Black gave the first James Madison Lecture at New York University School of Law. Although the Swarthmore speech reached only a small audience, the other two received national and international attention. Taken together they provided a full statement of Black's abiding faith in literal and absolute prescriptions as the basis for applying the Bill of Rights and the Constitution.

"Life without liberty" was not "worth living." History and the classics "proved" that the death of Socrates, the crucifixion of Jesus the "Great Dissenter," the conflicts culminating in Magna Carta, the persecution of seventeenth-century Puritan dissenter John Lilburne, and Madison's and the Founding Fathers' struggle resulting in independence and the Constitution were fundamentally no different from the human travails that forced Einstein to flee Hitler's tyranny. This unchanging human condition meant that the "desire of people to be free from government oppression" was the "same all over the world" throughout all time. The Constitution, he said, "with its absolute gurantees of individual rights," was the "best hope for the aspirations of freedom which men share everywhere." Governmental persecutions challenged the "basic assumptions" of the First Amendment that "our government should not, even for the best of motives, suppress criticism of the way public affairs are conducted," and that the nation's "security depends upon freedom of expression rather than upon suppression of expression."

Only through the "literal and unequivocal" reading of the entire Bill of Rights and the Constitution, moreover, was personal freedom attainable. Frankfurter's commitment to restraint meant that in First Amendment cases the Court often applied a balancing test. It also produced decisions involving the Fourteenth Amendment in which the states prevailed over individual rights. Black's conviction that human nature was changeless, however, led to an unswerving reliance on prescriptions and literalism as the surest guides to the application of the Court's authority. To many observers, the presumption of changeless human nature led Black to approach the First Amendment in a naive fashion. He did not , however, think so. Accordingly, if the Court accepted the presumption that the guarantees of the First Amendment were absolute, it could do neither more nor less than enforce those guarantees unequivocally. A literal reading of the First Amendment showed that the government could control certain conduct that *indirectly* affected personal expression, but it was the Court's responsibility to set forth and follow principles maintaining the distinction between conduct and absolutely protected expression.

Finally, in cases involving the due process clause, Black argued that the Court was bound to protect individual freedom from state interference up to, but not beyond, that point required by the Bill of Rights. Although supporters of both activism and restraint often agreed with Black on results in particular cases, they did not embrace his theory of total incorporation. Nevertheless, Black adamantly supported it as the surest way to restrict the Court's discretion while expanding the defense of individual liberty.

Black and his colleagues continued to exercise restraint toward the power of the New Deal regulatory state. The Court applied the commerce clause, taxing power, and innumerable federal laws, favoring increased delegation of congressional authority to manage the nation's growing economy to the President and bureaucrats. In an antitrust decision Black suggested how presumptive and complete had become big government's control of the economic order. Federal authorities could "presume conclusively," he said, that "certain agreements or practices" that had a "pernicious effect on competition" and lacked "any redeeming virtue" were "unreasonable and therefore illegal without elaborate inquiry as to the precise harm they have caused or the business excuse for their use."

During the mid-1950s Black also encountered difficulties at home. He was hospitalized because of serious complications arising from shingles. In 1955 further physical problems led Black to check into the Mayo Clinic. However, he played tennis as regularly as possible, and he had long since stopped smoking. In addition, Black kept up the habit of visiting Miami during the winter holidays. He helped all his children financially by liquidating some property in Birmingham. Although he reiterated how "very proud" he was of "each one of my children," he could not resist insisting that they remember that the gift represented "the labor" and "sacrifice" of himself and their mother.

Black concluded by voicing the hard-learned conviction: *"Don't get into debt for current living expenses. Such a course is the beginning of trouble."*

Eventually, Black's personal life acquired a new stability. After living for six years as a bachelor following the sudden death of Josephine, on September 11, 1957, Black married Elizabeth Seay DeMeritte, a native Alabamian who had worked for fifteen years as a secretary for the federal district court in Birmingham before becoming Black's executive assistant in 1955. About that time she and Fred E. DeMeritte agreed on an amicable divorce. Black urged on her a "reading program" to "develop a philosophy of life." As Black introduced her to his favorite classical and historical works, they grew closer, until she confided to her diary that he was "moving slowly toward marriage," though he "wanted to approach it analytically." Finally, he visited her to talk of "love and the Supreme Court," and two days later they were quietly married in Black's Alexandria home. He was seventy-one; she was forty-nine.

A particular "philosophy of life" shaped the justice's approach to American liberalism. He believed that self-respect was vital to preserving the interdependency between individual and community welfare; and the same assumption shaped his distinctive constitutional defense of liberalism. Even so he could not avoid the liberal dilemma. The Court's refusal to accept Black's prescriptive principles reflected an inability to establish clear guidelines governing the relationship between state and federal authority and the Bill of Rights. Big government had become permanent, but the limits of its power remained enmeshed in intractable conflict.

CHAPTER NINE

The Warren Court (1960–1968)

❖
❖

For Black, as for the nation, the 1960s were trying times. Despite recurrent criticism, his public stature increased as the administrations of John F. Kennedy and Lyndon B. Johnson brought the consummation of liberalism, while the Warren Court steadily expanded guarantees of individual rights. And yet massive social disorder, the assassinations of Kennedy, Martin Luther King, Jr., and Robert F. Kennedy, the triumph of Richard Nixon, and the dramatic rise of George Wallace and right-wing groups remained threats to liberalism. Amidst charges that he was retreating, Black defended the liberal faith and remained consistent in his constitutional prescriptions, continuing his effort to strike a balance between activism and self-restraint.

Black was gratified when Kennedy expanded the federal government's social welfare role. In addition to further increases in minimum wage and Social Security benefits, Kennedy won passage of subsidies for middle-income housing, mass transportation systems, and open space preservation. The most significant extension of federal assistance, however, came with Johnson's Great Society, which included medical aid for the elderly and younger welfare recipients under Medicare and Medicaid, as well as numerous educational, employment, and housing programs under the Office of Economic Opportunity and other agencies. The Secondary Education Act of 1965, despite the First Amendment's establishment clause, provided federal funding for public and private schools. Black's *Everson* decision of 1947 provided a constitutional basis for the law that aided needy students rather than the schools. As these and other policies became law, Black was proud of Johnson's record as President: "You have demonstrated beyond doubt your equal devotion to every part of our country and your determination to work towards the national goal of equal justice to all people, regardless of place, race, religion, or belief."

Black also consistently supported government regulation of the economy. In *Ferguson v. Skrupa* (1963) he reiterated the constitutional presumption that ordinarily the Court would exercise restraint toward government intervention. "Legislative bodies have broad scope to experiment with economic problems," he said. "Whether the legislature takes for its textbook Adam Smith, Herbert Spencer, Kord Keynes, or some other is no concern of ours." When Black supported the vigorous enforcement of antitrust laws, a *Fortune* editorial entitled "Anti-Trust in a Coonskin Cap" charged that his understanding of modern economics was old-fashioned. Nevertheless, a majority of the Court joined him in upholding pervasive federal authority.

The social turbulence of the 1960s, however, generated new challenges. To the South's massive resistance against integration, Martin Luther King, Jr., and others responded with a campaign of nonviolent, passive resistance. The growing emphasis on public demonstrations, and the corresponding and often brutal repression by officials in Oxford, Mississippi, and Birmingham and Selma, Alabama, resulted in still more disorder. Eventually, the conflict sufficiently aroused northern public opinion that shortly before his assassination Kennedy proposed vital civil rights legislation that was subsequently enacted and extended under Johnson. But new racial disorder erupted in northern ghettos, first in Harlem and then in Watts during the summers of 1964 and 1965. After King's assassination on April 4, 1968, the unrest climaxed in nationwide riots. Elizabeth remarked in her diary that "Hugo has been saying that the demonstrations would lead to riots and anarchy and he is borne out."

The growing resistance to the involvement in Vietnam also worried Black. Elizabeth described him as a "pacifist" concerning the Vietnam conflict. In 1965 shortly after Johnson announced a major increase in the number of troops he was sending to Vietnam, Black warned an advisor close to the President that "wars often cause defeats of Presidents." Again Elizabeth noted in her diary that Black's prophesy tragically came true. The antiwar conflict reached a climax in August 1968 with the bloodshed during the Chicago Democratic Convention.

The domestic disorder concerned Black for deeper reasons. The scale of unrest and the often vicious response of officials left Black wondering whether a majority might not ultimately endorse a more repressive government. He told Elizabeth that the "people in this country subconsciously want a change in government, since all seem to want a government by demonstrations and marching." Moreover, Black warned, "Hitler took to the streets before he took over."

He felt even more keenly because the unrest touched those closest to him. During the Selma clash a band of segregationists clubbed James Reeb, a white Unitarian minister, who died from the wounds. Reeb was a friend of the Black family; he had been the minister at Josephine's wedding. When Elizabeth asked Black whether they should send flowers, she wrote in her diary, "I got from Hugo almost a cry of agony and impatience, begging me not to bring it up again." If he does "what I ask, he says, and it's published, he will probably have to sit out all those cases."

This opposition to disorder was consistent with Black's conviction that individual rights depended on stable social relations and responsible behavior. Throughout his life, however, events had disrupted the proper balance. The danger arose not only from the government, but also from the people themselves, if they turned too readily to lawlessness. Black assured meetings of the Tuscaloosa and Birmingham bar associations that lawlessness could never produce a better society. Similarly, he told Elizabeth shortly before Congress passed the civil rights laws that the courts, though "not as glamorous as the streets," were the "route by which the only lasting civil rights will come."

Black's reaction altered and sometimes strained his relations with other justices. Tension surfaced regularly enough between Black and Douglas so that Elizabeth noted it with discomfort in her diary. In addition, Black began to advocate judicial self-restraint in certain civil liberties cases, which created conflict with the new majority favoring activism. Whittaker and Frankfurter had resigned in 1962, whereupon Kennedy replaced them with Denver lawyer Byron White and Secretary of Labor Arthur Goldberg. The resignations of Goldberg and Clark allowed Johnson to appoint his old friend and counselor Abe Fortas together with NAACP attorney and Solicitor General Thurgood Marshall.

Even Black and Warren disagreed on the limits of judicial activism. Since Warren had joined the Court, he and Black had shared a similar vision of American liberalism. When critics charged that Black's influence had changed Warren's views, Black emphasized the unity of their convictions. "He came into the Court with the same ideas I had," Black insisted. "He got them in California, I in Alabama." Nevertheless, throughout the 1960s Black found himself disagreeing with Warren on leading cases involving the expansion of the Bill of Rights.

Ironically, these fissures occurred at the very time the Court was under relentless attack. Conservatives within both political parties and right-wing groups such as the John Birch Society supported a campaign to impeach various justices. Black often received letters urging his impeachment because of decisions involving the civil rights movement and anti-Vietnam War demonstrators. Inevitably the letters linked these groups and the "Communist menance" bent on destroying America "from within." The communists sent "speakers to our colleges to teach their doctrines to our young people, they stir up racial troubles, they cause youth riots, they steal our defense secrets—yet they are protected by the great Supreme Court, which was formed to protect America, not some foreign ideology."

Black knew that this attack on the Court reflected profound emotions. "Sir, I am just a common laborer, without any influence, except to vote, and I use this to the best of my knowledge," said an anonymous letter writer. "I was very much afraid the communists would take over this country, because I have five small sons and I want to live in freedom." Such sentiments made the widespread disorder of the sixties particularly dangerous. However good the motives of demonstrators, the unrest aroused Americans' deepest anxieties and could lead to the election of those who would use fear to justify restricting liberty. Black perceived the initial steps in this direction during the state gubernatorial elections of 1966; he told Elizabeth that Ronald Reagan's victory in California over liberal Pat Brown was "bad." He thought the same of George Wallace's triumph through the election of his wife, Lurleen.

Black put his faith in an informed public's respect for the Constitution to prevent repression. Neither politicians nor publishers gave the southern people completely accurate reports of what the southern states could do consistent with their national responsibilities. he wrote in 1962. Misinformation fostered the same sort of fear, ignorance, and anger that had caused the Civil War. White Southerners needed to understand that devising "ways to defy and defeat the will of the Nation" would once "again bring on unnecessary pain and suffering." States could not prevent the "overwhelming majority" from living "true to their constitutional ideals of equal freedom for all." The foundation of the Constitution was a "belief that all people, whatever their color and whatever their history" were "human beings created by the same Creator, all entitled to have equal opportunities to do their part in helping to carry out the great national plan under which all our people must live." Black traced these convictions back to his boyhood: "I do not recall ever having heard anything contrary to them in my home," he said, "and I am sure that any Sunday school teachers in the little churches at Ashland, Alabama, came very near to expressing this same philosophy when they talked to me about the Sermon on the Mount and repeated the story of the Good Samaritan." America was "great" because the Constitution did not foster "slavery, hatred and a caste system" but instead was dedicated to the "principle of Equal Justice Under Law."

The turmoil of the sixties reflected the public's growing acceptance of extralegal action. Acquiescence in violence eventually produced a backlash. The victories of Reagan and Wallace resulted, he told his clerks, from human anxieties that "had been the problem since the time of Tacitus." However, he was sure that the constancy of human character also demonstrated the truth of Tacitus' observation that a people could "choose to maintain their greatness by justice rather than violence." The Court's chief responsibility was to encourage higher rather than lower sentiments in the people.

As disagreements with Douglas, Warren, and Fortas appeared, some observers argued that he was retreating from activism. The apparent shift, however, was a renewed emphasis upon community welfare. In the sixties, he continued to seek a balance between majoritarianism and liberty, and in the search for balance he relied on clear prescriptions. He hedged his famous assertion that the First Amendment's guarantee of speech was absolute by distinguishing pure speech from behavior such as picketing—which, though a form of expression, was conduct and therefore not protected absolutely. The distinction was like that between advocacy of action and overt action itself. The First Amendment permitted advocacy of controversial ideas until evidence proved that some unlawful act resulted. Similarly, Black held that the strict separation between church and state under the establishment clause did not preclude the state from providing safe transportation for both public and parochial schoolchildren. Since only economic and safety considerations determined eligibility for financial assistance, he said, on the issue of religion the state was neutral. Black's theory of incorporation thus balanced activism and restraint by limiting the state's power only to the point specifically required by the Bill of Rights.

Cases involving voting rights tested Black's consistency. Since the forties the Court had slowly but steadily undermined the southern exclusion of blacks from the polls. *Gomillion* v. *Lightfoot* (1960) represented the Court's growing defense of black voting rights. The Court overturned an Alabama law that enabled white city officials to establish boundaries excluding nearly all eligible black voters from Tuskegee municipal elections. Emphasizing that *Gomillion* involved racial injustice whereas the earlier decisions had not, Frankfurter agreed with Black's reversal. Shortly thereafter, Brennan got a 6–3 majority to go further in *Baker* v. *Carr* (1962). The case involved the impact of legislative malapportionment in three Tennessee cities. In a pathbreaking opinion, the Court upheld jurisdiction to consider the apportionment issue, returning the cases to the lower federal court for final decision. *Baker* precipitated a storm of criticism, climaxing in an unsuccessful proposal for a constitutional amendment removing jurisdiction in apportionment cases.

Baker prompted similar cases throughout the nation. *Wesberry* v. *Sanders* (1964) challenged a Georgia congressional district in which the representation of metropolitan Atlanta was proportionally less than that of less populated rural counties. After thoroughly reviewing the intent of the Constitution's Framers and the nation's English heritage, Black declared Georgia's plan invalid. For a six to three majority, he held that "construed in its historical context" the Constitution's "command" was that "as nearly as is practicable one man's vote in a congressional election is to be worth as much as another's." The Court extended Black's "one man, one vote" standard to state elections in *Reynolds* v. *Sims* (1964). Warren decided that "the Equal Protection Clause requires that both houses of a state legislature be apportioned on a population basis." The "basic constitutional principle of representative government" was, he said, "equality of population among districts."

The apportionment decisions were consistent in a general way with Black's constitutional faith. A Clay County childhood, public career in Birmingham, and tenure in the Senate taught him that Alabama's black belt maintained its dominance over the more populous northern part of the state primarily because of malapportionment. Black disenfranchisement and the underrepresentation of white voters in places such as Birmingham were linked.

Critics were unconvinced. There was no historical evidence that the Framers of the Constitution advocated the sort of equal representation embodied in the prhase "one man, one vote." They had specifically granted states equal representation in the Senate, denying altogether the relevance of population. Moreover, although the provision governing the lower house reads "Each House shall be the Judge of the Elections, Returns and Qualifications of its members," the Court's new standard limited that authority. At the very least, Black's reading of the Framers was idealized. Black's opinion, like the rest of the reapportionment revolution, accordingly violated the principle of judicial self-restraint and undermined the separation of powers.

Nevertheless, after 1965 Black's stand became more complex. Despite *Gomillion* the Civil Rights Commission reported 100 Deep South counties in which fewer than 10 percent of the eligible black residents were registered to vote. In order to stop the persistent policy of intimidation and harassment, the 1965 legislation provided for comprehensive federal intervention to protect black voters. The law automatically suspended literacy and educational tests where the U.S. Attorney General found that fewer than 50 percent of otherwise eligible residents were registered or had voted in the presidential election of 1964. The suspension remained effective for five years, and was not subject to challenge in court. In addition, the law authorized the attorney general to assist in the selection of federal "examiners" to supervise elections in states with a history of violating the Fifteenth Amendment. In its most radical departure from precedent, the act also required that before states could change franchise practices, prior approval was necessary from either the Attorney General or the federal court of the District of Columbia.

Black's support for the Voting Rights Act was equivocal. Warren rejected the claims of South Carolina, Alabama, and several other states in *South Carolina* v. *Katzenbach* that the law's provisions suspending literacy and other voting tests, compelling preclearance, and establishing federal examiners went beyond powers granted to Congress under the Fifteenth Amendment. Black agreed with "substantially all" the decision except that upholding the requirement of preclearance. Reviewing the debates of the Constitutional Convention of 1787 and other sources, Black objected that the preclearance proviso violated the proper division between state and national power. Black believed that the objectionable provision forced the states to "entreat federal authorities in far away places for approval of local laws before they can become effective," creating the "impression that the State or States" were "little more than conquered provinces." In effect, this gave the Attorney General or federal court a veto power over state laws that the framers of the Constitution had denied categorically to Congress. Such authority violated the "long-established principle" that civil rights challenges should arise only "once an operative state law has created an actual case and controversy." Moreover, preclearance approached "dangerously near to wiping the States out as useful and effective units."

Black's opinion in *South Carolina* v. *Katzenbach* revealed his persistent—but increasingly difficult—struggle to reconcile activism and restraint. He had always supported judicial protection of the voting rights of both white and black Americans. He also favored congressional enactment of voting rights legislation in 1957, 1960, and 1965. However, preclearance limited the judicial remedy vital to sustaining federal authority, and the requirement of prior authorization discouraged state attempts to remedy racial disenfranchisement on their own. This in turn undercut white Southerners' self-respect, breeding resentment and resistance.

Black attempted further to prescribe the limits of judicial activism in *Harper* v. *Virginia* (1966). For a 6 to 3 majority Douglas struck down the state's poll tax as a violation of the equal protection clause—reversing a 1937 decision. The Court declared that because the poll tax introduced "wealth or payment of a fee as a measure of a voter's qualification" it was "an invidious discrimination." Black dissented. Noting that he had concurred in the unanimous 1937 opinion, he nonetheless emphasized that had racial discrimination been at issue in *Harper,* he would have voted with the majority. Since it was not, however, Black argued that the Court should have adhered to precedent and exercised self-restraint. He "disliked" the poll tax but preferred to have Congress end it instead of using the equal protection clause to write into the Constitution the Court's "own notion of good governmental policy."

Harper was consistent with Black's effort to balance restraint and activism and with the position he had maintained as both a senator and justice: legislation was better than a Court ruling to resolve any "invidious discrimination" arising from the poll tax. A fairly administered tax encouraged good citizenship and participatory democracy; people who paid were likely to have a far greater interest in their government. Ultimately, he opposed the Court's activism because it jeopardized the citizen's stake in public affairs.

Other cases involving racial justice challenged Black's ability to establish constitutional prescriptions governing activism and restraint. When Virginia school officials argued that the ambiguous standard of *Brown* II justified further delays in desegregation, Black held in *Griffin* v. *Prince Edward County* (1964) that the "time for mere 'deliberate speed' has run out." Meanwhile, starting in 1960 black youths began "sit-in" protests at segregated eating and retail establishments by requesting service and refusing to leave until the authorities intervened. The sit-ins challenged the Court's distinction between private and state action. Since the 1940s the Court had consistently applied the Fourteenth Amendment to overturn racial segregation imposed by the state, but it never questioned that private individuals could refuse to associate with those of another race. Thus in the restrictive covenant, white primary, and *Jaybird* cases the Court struck down private discrimination only because it was inextricably entwined with maintaining state-mandated racial discrimination.

For Douglas, the sit-ins raised the question whether public officials could constitutionally enforce private discrimination, thereby putting "a racial cordon around businesses serving the public. If they can do it in the restaurant cases, they can do it in drug stores, private hospitals and common carriers." Black's view was more restricted. He readily acknowledged that Congress or a state could enact a law forbidding racial discrimination even in private businesses. Recalling his "Pappy's" store in Ashland, however, Black declared further that, "I don't think the Constitution forbids the owner of a store to keep people out," so long as the business was "really wholly your own and neither in its origin nor in its maintenance" was involved "directly or indirectly" in issues of state or federal authority.

The conflict within the Court became increasingly irreconcilable. In several early cases the Court, including Black, overturned convictions of protestors where discrimination by private businesses involved state action. But *Bell* v. *Maryland* (1964) asked the Court to determine whether the eviction of civil rights demonstrators from a private Baltimore restaurant violated the First and Fourteenth amendments. A majority agreed that there was no direct state action as usually defined, and the Court merely returned the case to state courts for trial in light of a new Maryland law—passed after the convictions—forbidding restaurants to deny individuals service for reasons of race.

Black was one of six justices expressing views in *Bell,* arguing that the Fourteenth Amendment did not "compel either a black man or a white man running his own private business to trade with anyone else against his will." He also dismised the demonstrators' claim that the First Amendment protected their behavior. The litigants "had a constitutional right to express" their views "wherever they had an unquestioned legal right to be." But the "right to freedom of expression is a right to express views—not a right to force other people to supply a platform or a pulpit" on private property. Finally, Black asserted, the principle of "liberty and equality for all" meant that the Constitution did not "confer upon any group the right to substitute rule by force for rule by law."

Almost immediately, however, Black's opposition became moot. The Civil Rights Act of 1964, prohibiting racial discrimination in restaurants and other public accommodations, relied on the commerce clause to enforce federal power; now that authority was aligned against racial injustice.

Black supported two decisions that demonstrated just how far federal intervention reached. Ollie's Barbeque, a Birmingham restaurant miles from any national highway, discriminated against blacks. Civil rights supporters sued, and the proprietor responded that his establishment lay outside the reach of the commerce clause. Nevertheless, the Court upheld the exercise of the commerce power, emphasizing that at least half of the restaurant's food products came through interstate trade. Similarly, the Court held that the commerce clause sanctioned the prohibition of racial discrimination in hotels or motels that served interstate travelers.

In First Amendment cases Black argued for absolute protection in suits involving what he regarded as traditional speech. *New York Times* v. *Sullivan* (1964) raised the issue whether state libel laws barred publication of political advertisements with minor factual errors revealing official interference with civil rights. A unanimous Court overturned convictions under an Alabama statute, holding that the First Amendment guaranteed publication of such advertisements criticizing public authorities unless a false statement was made "with knowledge that it was false or with reckless disregard of whether it was false or not." Black's concurring opinion asserted that the First and Fourteenth amendments provided the *Times* an "absolute, unconditional constitutional right to publish" its "criticism of the Montgomery agencies and officials."

Black also attempted to set the boundary between the First Amendment's absolute guarantees and conduct even when it came to obscenity. In *Ginzburg* v. *U.S.* (1966) he denied that the federal government had any power whatever to put any burden on speech and expression of ideas of any kind (as distinguished from conduct). In *Cox* v. *Louisiana* (1965) he agreed to overturn the conviction of civil rights activists who had demonstrated before a local courthouse. But he had "no doubt" that the state had the "power to protect judges, jurors, witnesses, and court officers from intimidation by crowds" seeking "to influence them by picketing, patrolling, or parading in or near the courthouses in which they do their business or the homes in which they live."

Black remained consistent on the establishment clause. *Engel* v. *Vitale* (1962) involved a New York law establishing in public school classrooms daily observance of a brief, nondenominational prayer, with voluntary individual participation. Several parents challenged the law as a violation of the First Amendment. Black's majority opinion declared the law invalid, for it mandated a clear religious preference. The support of government thus created "indirect coercive pressure upon religious minorities to conform to the prevailing officially approved religion." The Framers based the establishment clause "upon an awareness of the historical fact that governmentally established religions and religious persecutions go hand in hand." Religion was "too personal, too sacred, too holy, to permit its unhallowed perversion by a civil magistrate."

Opponents of the decision emphasized that the Constitution mentioned religion only twice, in the provision prohibiting tests as a qualification for federal office and in the First Amendment's establishment clause. Neither denied local school boards the authority to establish prayers. Moreover, little historical evidence supported Black's contention concerning the intentions of those who framed the establishment clause. As a result, the critics argued, Black's opinion was an unwarranted exercise of judicial activism.

Black responded that he had preserved the welfare of the community by protecting the rights of religious minorities. He remained consistent in this view by dissenting when the Court in 1968 upheld a New York law providing free textbooks to children in both public and private schools.

Black also remained steadfast in his theory of total incorporation, which the Court never fully accepted. The Court did expand the Bill of Rights guarantees applicable to the states under the due process clause: in the pathbreaking decisions of *Mapp* v. *Ohio* (1961), *Escobedo* v. *Illinois* (1964), and *Miranda* v. *Arizona* (1966) it declared that the Fourth Amendment's proscription of unwarranted search and seizures, the Sixth Amendment's right to counsel, and the Fifth Amendment's provision against self-incrimination all controlled state trials and police conduct. Black supported each of these opinions, and contributed one himself in *Gideon* v. *Wainwright* (1963). Selective rather than full incorporation triumphed, a result consistent with the spirit if not the letter of Black's theory.

The Court's imposition of national standards upon local law enforcement authorities was central to Richard Nixon's presidential campaign. Nixon exclaimed repeatedly that the Court's decisions had "gone too far in weakening the peace forces as against the criminal forces of this country." Black, however, struggled to establish the incorporation principle primarily because he believed that uniform constitutional rules controlling state police and courts would improve law enforcement. "Having served as a prosecutor myself for so long a time," he replied to a letter from a prosecuting attorney in Indiana, "I have great sympathy with efforts of prosecuting officers to enforce the law of the States and Nation."

Griswold v. *Connecticut* (1965) revealed, however, the limits of Black's constitutional principle. A state law prohibited the use of contraceptives and the distribution of birth control information to married couples. Douglas wrote the Court's decision, holding that the law violated a "marital right of privacy" implicit in the First, Fourth, and Fifth amendments and the due process clause. Black vigorously dissented. The right of privacy represented "a loose, flexible, uncontrolled standard for holding laws unconstitutional," suggested "an unrestrained judicial control as to the wisdom of legislative enactment," and jeopardized the "separation of governmental powers that the Framers set up." The Court had transcended Black's presumption that it should apply the Amendments as fully as, but no further than, a literal reading established.

Criticism of judicial activism helped give Nixon the lead in the 1968 campaign for the presidency. In addition, the conservative coalition of Republicans and southern Democrats blocked Johnson's attempted appointment of Fortas as chief justice after Warren announced his decision to retire. The defeat of Fortas involved more than political partisanship alone. Warren had said that he would remain as chief justice until the President chose a successor. Although Warren denied it was his intent, critics charged that he was attempting to pressure the Senate to accept a lame-duck president's liberal nominee, thus denying Nixon the opportunity to chose a conservative. Then rumors spread that Black and Douglas were also considering retirement. Indeed, Black's eyesight problems led Elizabeth to urge retirement. In February 1968, Black was eighty-two. Although he regularly played tennis and otherwise remained active, his eyesight gradually had declined until he could no longer safely drive a car. An operation improved the problem, but the slow loss of control heightened Black's concern about the inevitable. Periodically, he expressed the hope that if "he went first," Elizabeth would arrange for burial next to him when "her time came."

Various events were to shape Black's decision about retirement. The success of his Carpentier Lectures at Columbia University, delivered during the spring of 1968 before a standing-room audience of more than 1500, demonstrated that his mind remained sharp. Meanwhile, Nixon's narrow victory over Black's candidate, Hubert Humphrey, as well as Wallace's surprising showing, confirmed Black's fears that the social disorder of the sixties had created a popular mood threatening American liberalism. His continuing intellectual vigor, combined with the conviction that he could help forestall liberalism's decline, kept him on the Court.

CHAPTER TEN

The Vietnam Terminus (1968–1971)

❖
❖

The initial impact of Nixon's election on liberalism was uncertain. The Warren Court remained intact, and the means existed to extend liberal policies further. Black resisted the continuous expansion of executive authority and began to resist the judicial activism it had spawned. He did not waver from his constitutional faith once the Warren era ended. Ultimately, however, his advancing years posed the gravest challenge he had ever known.

Not since the clash over the New Deal was the Supreme Court such a storm center. A writer for *The New Yorker* observed that "Mr. Nixon's attacks on the Court undoubtedly helped him win." Persistent urban racial violence weakened public sympathy for the civil rights movement. To most voters, these disturbances were part of the larger, more painful and divisive struggle over Vietnam. This confrontation in turn aroused deep tensions between adults and youths as opposition to Vietnam often became associated with controversial lifestyles, values, and behavior. To many Americans Nixon's contention that the Supreme Court's vigorous defense of individual rights was a primary cause of unrest rang true. His insistence that he would appoint only judges who believed in judicial self-restraint seemed compelling. Although old Roosevelt liberals such as Black rejected Nixon's criticism of the Court, they were nonetheless troubled.

As eight years of liberal presidencies ended, Black publicly addressed the tensions in a one-hour CBS news special in which journalists Eric Sevareid and Martin Agronsky interviewed the justice. Although CBS taped the program late in September 1968, it did not appear on the air until after the election. When the interviewers raised the "public clamor" involving the Court and the "notion" that its decisions had somehow restricted police and aided criminals, Black responded without hesitation. "Well, the Court didn't do it," he said. "No, the Constitution-makers did it. They were the ones that put in no man should be compelled to convict himself." And Black made clear his conviction that the Court's enforcement of the Framers' intent was correct. "Certainly, why shouldn't they?" he said. "Why did they write the Bill of Rights? They practically all relate to the ways cases shall be tried. And practically all of them make it more difficult to convict people of crime."

The millions of television viewers also learned of the limits Black placed upon individual rights. "Now the government would be in a very bad fix, I think, if the Constitution provided that" it was "without power to keep people" from "demonstrating or singing because they wanted to protest the government." Individuals had therefore only "a right to talk" where they had "a right to be, under valid laws." Here Black reiterated the distinction between speech, which was absolutely protected, and conduct, which was not. At the same time he explained why he advocated extending this absolute guarantee to pornography. The community could not agree on what was pornographic. The best safeguard against unacceptable contact with offensive material was, Black observed, the family's teaching of appropriate values to children. Parents "ought" to take care of their "children and warn them against things themselves rather than try to pass a law." If parents did their duty, children would have the strength of character to reject the obscene, as Black himself had done because of his upbringing.

Running throughout the CBS interview was Black's view of the Court's role in interpreting the Constitution. Black conceded that "our system" placed different individuals on the Court who in turn had different views of the proper judicial function. His duty was to follow as nearly as possible the literal meaning of the Constitution's words. In so doing he looked to the Framers for guidance, to the historical context in which they worked, and only then did he exercise his own judgment. The Framers knew intimately history's "long series of oppressions" and wrote the Constitution to "control the government," thereby limiting the perpetuation of oppression in the future.

He rejected the idea that judges should keep the Constitution in tune with the times. Since human behavior remained constant, principles of one age could govern another. Because most Americans did not understand the Constitution, however, the judges were bound to educate the public by articulating clear prescriptions. He conceded that the judges of the Supreme Court also sometimes failed at this. Black particularly regretted that the ambiguity of the "deliberate speed" standard in *Brown* II fostered resistance to the Court's original *Brown* decision.

The public response to Black's CBS interview was quite favorable. CBS spokesmen reported that they received over 100,000 requests for pocket-sized copies of the Constitution of the sort Black always carried with him and had mentioned during the program. The show received the Emmy Award for the year's best documentary. Although a majority of voters clearly questioned the Warren Court's vigorous defense of personal freedom, many Americans accepted Black's rationale for the Court's action.

About the same time that CBS aired the interview, Black's 1968 Columbia lectures were published as *A Constitutional Faith*. The book developed more fully the ideas discussed in the television show. The "heart" of the Constitution and the Bill of Rights was the First Amendment, he said, and it fostered among Americans "a sturdy and self-reliant character which is best for them and best for their government." The purpose of the Amendment was to give free individuals "so great an influence over the government's affairs that our society could abandon the age-old device of settling controversies through strife which leads inevitably to hatreds and bloodshed, and substitute for strife settlements by and through the peaceful agencies of government and law."

Pondering his "long journey from a frontier farmhouse in the hills of Clay County, Alabama, to the United States Supreme Court," Black felt his heart fill with gratitude and devotion to the Constitution which made his public life possible. The Constitution was his "legal bible." "I cherish every word of it, from the first to the last, and I personally deplore even the slightest deviation from its least important commands."

During this period, Black voted consistently with the majority to expand federal economic policies, particularly the application of the Fair Labor Standards Act to the states. Similarly, he was with the Court in extending the "one man, one vote" standard to the apportionment of local electoral districts. In *Benton* v. *Maryland* (1969), moreover, Black's incorporation theory received further, if still incomplete, approval. Thurgood Marshall held for six justices (including Black) that the double jeopardy clause of the Fifth Amendment applied to the states through the Fourteenth Amendment's due process clause. Yet, he dissented when the Court limited the state's authority in criminal cases as contrary to the Fourth Amendment's proscription of unreasonable searches and seizures. Black also joined Warren in dissent when the Court decided that state rules requiring one year's residence to qualify for welfare violated the equal protection clause.

Black's most conspicuous break with the Warren Court's activism occurred in the *Tinker* case. Late in 1965, three teenagers expressed their disagreement with the government's Vietnam policy by wearing black armbands to school. The principals of the Des Moines, Iowa, schools prohibited the planned action. The three attended classes; no significant interference with school activities resulted. School officials, however, enforced the new policy, suspending the three. Through their fathers the teenagers petitioned the federal district court, seeking an injunction restraining the school authorities from instituting the disciplinary procedure and seeking nominal damages. In due course a federal district court dismissed the complaint.

In February 1969 a majority of the Supreme Court reversed the district court's decision. Justice Abe Fortas noted that the youths' conduct resulted in no disturbance in school activities nor interference with the rights of other students. Under the Constitution, he went on, "free speech is not a right that is given only to be so circumscribed that it exists in principle but not in fact. Freedom of expression would not truly exist if the right could be exercised only in an area that a benevolent government has provided as a safe haven for crackpots."

These were the views to which Black dissented. He conceded that although he had "always believed" that under the First and Fourteenth amendments neither the federal nor state governments had "any authority to regulate or censor the content of speech," he had "never believed that any person has a right to give speeches or engage in demonstrations where he pleases and when he pleases." The Court's majority opinion pushed free expression beyond proper limits, undercutting traditional sources of order. "School discipline, like parental discipline, is an integral and important part of training our children to be good citizens—to be better citizens." Following the Court's holding, he predicted that "some students" in "all schools will be ready, able, and willing to defy their teachers on practically all orders." Groups of students all over the land were already "running loose, conducting break-ins, sit-ins, lie-ins, and smash-ins." More particularly, Black reiterated his distinction between speech and conduct. The First Amendment guaranteed the "right to think, speak, and write freely without governmental censorship or interference." Where there was more action than speech, however, the democratic system of government that free debate made possible was subverted. He had "always been careful to draw a line between speech and conduct," he wrote in *A Constitutional Faith,* the year *Tinker* came to the Court. Social order, no less than vigorous written and spoken expression, was essential to democracy. Unrestrained conduct too easily disintegrated into disorder, and "the crowds that press in the streets for noble goals today can be supplanted tomorrow by street mobs pressuring" for "precisely opposite ends."

He thus acknowledged the limits of the absolute defense of free expression that he had proclaimed during the McCarthy era, when anticommunist prosecutions excluded controversial ideas from the intellectual marketplace. The resulting fear, ignorance, and guilt by association undermined democracy and faith in constitutional rights. Americans would have rejected the communists' ideas if given the opportunity to consider them objectively. Such evaluation, in turn, would have strengthened both the public's faith in democracy and respect for individual rights.

The symbolic protest in *Tinker* expressed a similar attitude from an opposite direction. Despite evidence claiming the contrary, the protestors' armbands disrupted the educational process. Students could not concentrate on "lesser issues" when "black armbands" were "ostentatiously displayed" to draw "attention to the wounded and dead of the war, some of the wounded and the dead being their friends and neighbors." In light of the period's massive unrest, Black believed that the armband protest undermined the orderly discourse in the classroom essential to both community stability and individual rights.

The justices' split over *Tinker* was symptomatic of more profound troubles engulfing the Warren Court. President-elect Nixon had requested that Warren finish the Court's current term, leaving the precise time of departure indefinite. On May 5, 1969, however, the media revealed various private transactions between Fortas and a businessman convicted of illegal stock practices. The public uproar fell upon a Court already shaken by Nixon's criticism. Shortly thereafter Fortas resigned. Less than a week later Nixon announced the nomination of, and the Senate readily confirmed, federal circuit judge Warren E. Burger to be chief justice of the Supreme Court. The following month Nixon nominated federal circuit judge Clement Haynesworth to succeed Fortas as associate justice, but the Senate refused confirmation. The Senate also rejected the President's nomination of federal appellate judge Harold Carswell, but confirmed federal judge Harry Blackmun to fill the seat vacated by Fortas.

During the summer of 1969 Black experienced another private travail. During a tennis game with Elizabeth, "he kind of wobbled off the tennis court and sat down," and could not "call his grandchildren by name." The days passed and impaired memory continued. He discussed with Elizabeth the "errors people make, and his biggest one was joining the Klan." Although there was gradual recovery from the minor stroke, Elizabeth perceived that "Hugo himself seems not to realize that his mentality has been impaired." It made her realize that she did not want him to remain on the Court with less than his whole mentality. By October, however, recovery seemed complete, and Black began his thirty-third year as a justice.

Meanwhile, an academic observer charged that he had retreated from liberalism. Referring to the CBS interview, Professor Glendon Schubert contrasted the "well-informed, sensitive and liberal" commentators with the "rigid, crochety, dogmatic old man." The *Tinker* dissent suggested, moreover, that increasing conservatism resulted from a "cultural obsolescence" and "psychophysiological senescence." Schubert argued that it was "a supreme irony that Hugo Black's problem is that he has become too old for the job," given that age was "precisely Franklin Roosevelt's complaint against the Hughes Court, and it was to break the grip of gerontocracy upon the Supreme Court that Black was appointed to it."

Yale law professor Alexander Bickel had a more subtle view. Despite his rigorous criticism of the Warren Court's judicial activism, Bickel asserted that "another classification is needed for Mr. Justice Black," who was "magnificent in old age and wedded to the sacred text of the Constitution." He implied that the consistency in Black's opinions derived from his struggle to establish clear prescriptions governing the limits of activism and restraint, based upon original intent, literalism, and history.

Black addressed Nixon's relaxation of desegregation enforcement in *Alexander* v. *Board of Education* (1969). On the basis of the *Brown* II principle of "deliberate speed," Justice Department and HEW officials requested that the Fifth Circuit Court of Appeals postpone implementing a decree for immediate desegregation of Mississippi schools. When the case reached the Supreme Court Black threatened to dissent if the justices did not end the government's delay and return to the original order. "The duty of this Court and of the others is too simple to require perpetual litigation and deliberation," he wrote in a memo to the other justices. That "duty" was to "extirpate all racial discrimination from our system of public schools NOW." A few days later the Court handed down a unanimous order, declaring "effective immediately'" that the "continued operation of segregated schools under a standard of allowing 'all deliberate speed' for desegregation was no longer constitutionally permissible."

In the pathbreaking *Swann* decision of 1971, the Court held that courts could order busing to improve racial balance in public schools. The opinion met massive popular opposition. Indeed, the issue so profoundly divided the Court that, privately, Black threatened to dissent; "I strongly disagree" that "federal courts may order school boards to transport students across cities to balance schools racially or to eliminate one race schools which have resulted from private residential patterns rather than school board imposed segregation." Moreover, he said that the Constitution did not "require racial balance." Despite such strong language, Black conceded that flexibility was vital in order to eliminate state-mandated segregation. Policies such as busing were permissible so long as no rigid percentage of racial mix was required. The Court accepted this principle and reached its unanimous decision. Nixon responded, however, by supporting a constitutional amendment prohibiting busing and by advocating federal aid to private schools.

Black also established prescriptions to apply to the antiwar unrest arising from Nixon's escalation of the Vietnam conflict. The government won a conviction of Elliott Ashton Welsh for refusing induction into the armed forces. Welsh claimed the status of conscientious objector on the ground that he opposed participation in any war because killing was morally wrong. Since this belief was not religious in nature—the traditional ground for conscientious objection—the federal judge ordered Welsh imprisoned for violating the Selective Service Act. On appeal, a severely divided Supreme Curt reversed the judgment. Black held that the test for determining the validity of conscientious-objector claims was whether "opposition to war stemmed from moral, ethical, or religious beliefs" maintained with the "strength of traditional religious convictions."

Since his days as an Alabama lawyer, police court judge, and prosecutor, Black had trusted in juries to reconcile conflicting public attitudes. At the same time, he relied on explicit guidelines for the jury's judgment. In a case arising from Robert Toussie's refusal to register for the draft, Black's majority opinion reversed the conviction resulting from a jury trial. The issue was whether the conviction should stand in light of the draft law's statute of limitations. "There was no doubt that the jury found" that Toussie "willfully failed to register and thereby subject himself to the same possibility of military service that faces other young men who fully comply with their legal obligations," Black said for a divided Court. However, the law not only made the failure to register a crime, it also "made prosecution of such offenses subject to the statute of limitations." Although the lawful obligation to comply with the statute of limitations "may permit a rogue to escape," when a court found that such a law barred a "given prosecution, it must give effect to the clear expression of congressional will" that "no person shall be prosecuted, tried, or punished."

In more ordinary state criminal cases, meanwhile, Black supported the jury. He had consistently advocated extending the protections of the Fifth and Sixth amendments under the theory of total incorporation, but resisted enlarging the Fourth Amendment's prohibition of unreasonable searches and seizures. His Alabama legal experience convinced him that the guarantee against self-incrimination and the right to counsel would limit abuse while ensuring the effectiveness of the authorities. The Fourth Amendment's reasonableness standard was too vague to maintain this vital balance.

In *Whiteley* v. *Warden* (1971), however, the Court rejected Black's reasoning. It reversed a jury verdict against a burglar whose conviction rested in part upon evidence obtained under circumstances deemed unreasonable. Dissenting, Black asserted that the "Fourth Amendment itself does not expressly command that evidence obtained by its infraction should always be excluded from proof." Consequently, there was "not even a suspicion here that this hardened criminal is innocent and I would let him stay in confinement to serve his sentence."

Black advocated further reconciliation of state and federal authority in the administration of social welfare. In *Goldberg* v. *Kelly* (1970) the Court overturned a state's cutoff of public assistance, holding that such action required a post-termination hearing. A 5–4 majority declared that the state had violated the due process clause of the Fourteenth Amendment. Black dissented, arguing against an unwarranted exercise of judicial activism. Central to Black's total incorporation theory was the necessity of limiting the Court's discretionary judgment while enlarging its duty to apply the literal provisions of the Bill of Rights. Although Black was in the minority in the *Goldberg* case, he voted with the majority upholding another state's limitation of other welfare programs, despite claims that such a policy violated the equal protection clause.

Since joining the Court in 1937 Black had supported judicial restraint in favor of laws involving economic or social welfare. Moreover, he suggested in his *Goldberg* dissent that the government's combined Vietnam-era military and social expenditures had threatened to spawn inflation.

Black struggled to diminish the popular animosity sustaining Nixon's opposition to the Court by encouraging judicial self-restraint in other areas. After the *Griswold* decision of 1965, controversy arose over whether the right of privacy included a woman's right to have an abortion. Nixon sided with anti-abortion advocates, significantly restricting the grounds on which female military personnel could request abortions. In *U.S.* v. *Vuitch* (1971), Black construed narrowly a District of Columbia anti-abortion statute, while refusing to consider the privacy principle he had opposed in *Griswold*. The decision shifted the burden of proof from the individual to the government, thereby establishing a "most liberal abortion" law.

Meanwhile, in *Younger* v. *Harris* (1971), Black denied federal court authority to release a radical antiwar protester while his jury trial was underway in a state tribunal. In civil rights cases where it was clear that the prejudice of local juries prevented a fair trial, the Court had permitted such intervention. Black found no such discrimination in *Younger,* thereby upholding in sweeping terms state jury-trial prosecutions of radicals. Black also sustained a federal voting law extending the franchise to eighteen-year-olds but rejected the contention that states were constitutionally bound to do the same.

In the most dramatic case, Black sided with the Court's majority against Nixon's assertion of power. As the national turmoil over Vietnam continued, the *New York Times* and other newspapers published the "Pentagon Papers." Leaked covertly to the press, these classified government documents revealed troubling distortions in the government's account of the nation's involvement in Vietnam. Claiming that publication threatened national security, the Nixon administration sought an injunction. In a special summer session the Court, by a 6 to 3 vote, rejected the government's claim. Black's concurring opinion affirmed an absolutist reading of the First Amendment. "And paramount among the responsibilities of a free press," he exclaimed, "is the duty to prevent any part of the government from deceiving the people and sending them off to distant lands to die of foreign fevers and foreign shot and shell." "The greater the importance of safe-guarding the community from incitement to the overthrow of our institutions," Black said, the "more imperative is the need to preserve inviolate the constitutional rights of free speech, free press, and free assembly." This was the "security of the Republic, the very foundation of constitutional government."

During Burger's initial tenure, then, Black applied his old constitutional faith to maintain the interdependency of community welfare and individual rights against the reaction that he perceived Nixon as representing. And yet Black knew, too, that Nixon had tapped American voters' anger and fear stemming from the protests, the crimes associated with young people's rebellion and racial unrest, and inflation. The resulting alienation undermined the self-respect on which democracy depended. Black suggested the depth of this concern in marginal notes that he scribbled as he read a critique of contemporary America, *The Greening of America,* by his former law clerk, Charles A. Reich. To Reich's argument that the American dream of individual freedom and opportunity was "lost" and "destroyed," Black responded, "I do not agree," and "It is not yet destroyed." Reich denied that "success is determined by character, morality, hard work, and self denial"; Black countered, "no." As for Reich's charge that government and society were "impervious to democratic or popular control," forming an "immensely powerful machine, ordered, legalistic, rational, yet utterly out of human control, wholly and perfectly indifferent to any human values," Black reacted "it does not seem so to me," and "I think not."

The opinion in the *Pentagon Papers* case was the last pronouncement Black delivered from the Supreme Court. He became increasingly frail during the spring and summer of 1971. By late August his resignation from the Court seemed inevitable. At the end of August, Elizabeth and Hugo, Jr., helped Black prepare a letter of resignation. At his father's direction, the son also began destroying the justice's conference notes, though the rest of his papers were preserved. During the same period, Justice John Harlan (hospitalized in the room next to Black's) learned that his illness was terminal. On September 17 Black submitted his resignation to Nixon, as did Harlan several days later. Following another stroke Black was listed as being in serious condition; early in the morning of September 25 he died.

Black's funeral embodied elements that had sustained and shaped a life that transcended personal experience to influence the whole nation. A rough-hewn casket of Alabama scrub pine recalled the beliefs acquired in his Clay County youth. Baptist hymns and readings from the Psalms and Corinthians, followed by an epitaph from Virgil, echoed the sources Black had drawn upon as lawyer, elected official, and judge to reach the hearts and minds of his fellow countrymen. In death, as in life, he carried a pocket-sized copy of the Constitution.

The bell of Washington's National Cathedral tolled eighty-five times, one for each year of a life that had begun in the era of rural protest and progressive reform, attained maturity during the triumph of New Deal liberalism, and ended amid the reaction against the sixties and the Vietnam struggle. The view from his grave in Arlington National Cemetery was of Washington. As senator and justice, Black had helped to make the city central to the life of every American. Yet he also fought for the ideal of individual liberty and stood for the distrust of big government, both embodied in the Jefferson Memorial.

After all, perhaps the hope expressed in his epitaph was fulfilled. May I "dwell remote from care, master of myself, and under no necessity of doing everyday what my heart condemns. Let me no more be seen at the wrangling bar, a pale and anxious candidate for precarious fame." Finally at rest, Black found what he had never sought in life, release from the struggle for self-respect and freedom.

A Note on the Sources

Hugo L. Black was a fairly careful recordkeeper, though his view concerning what should be preserved was ambivalent. As his health deteriorated during the last weeks of life, Black saw to it that his notes recording thirty-four years of the Court's private conferences were destroyed. He believed these notes presented a distorted view of the conference process, since they represented the votes and opinions of only one justice and were often changed or modified in subsequent discussions. At the same time, Black saved a remarkable number of personal papers that provided useful information about his legal and public career in Birmingham, service as a Senator from Alabama, and tenure as associate justice. This material includes not only private memoranda and commentary on substantive issues but also extensive correspondence with family members, associates, colleagues, and others giving invaluable insight into Black's family life and professional relations. The Black Papers are well catalogued in the Twentieth Century Collection of the Manuscripts Division of the Library of Congress.

I also examined the Felix Frankfurter and Louis Brandeis Papers at the Manuscripts Division of Harvard Law School. Other useful collections are the Stanley Reed Papers at Harvard Law School and the Court papers of justices William O. Douglas and William J. Brennan, Jr., and Chief Justice Earl Warren at the Library of Congress.

Of particular value regarding Black's personal life is the correspondence with his son, Hugo, Jr., in the Black Papers and the diary of Elizabeth Black published under the title: *Mr. Justice and Mrs. Black, the Memoirs of Hugo L. Black and Elizabeth Black* (New York, 1986). The "Memoirs" the justice wrote during his later years, published for the first time as part of Mrs. Black's book, provide information about his Clay County youth and career in Birmingham to 1926. Hugo Black, Jr., *My Father: A Remembrance*

(New York, 1975), and Virginia Foster Durr, *Outside the Magic Circle: The Autobiography of Virginia Foster Durr* (Tuscaloosa, 1985), suggest further perspectives from the point of view of his son and sister-in-law.

Gerald T. Dunne, *Hugo Black and the Judicial Revolution* (New York, 1977), is the only full biography of Black. The essays by various authors edited by Stephen Parks Strickland, entitled *Hugo Black and the Supreme Court: A Symposium* (Indianapolis, 1967), include excellent discussions of Black's constitutional faith considered in light of his life and career. Collections of Black's opinions that have introductory essays containing valuable biographical information are: John P. Frank, *Mr. Justice Black* (New York, 1949) and Irving Dilliard, *One Man's Stand for Freedom: Mr. Justice Black and the Bill of Rights* (New York, 1963). Another excellent selection of essays by distinguished authors, entitled "Mr. Justice Black: A Symposium," was published in 9 *Southwestern Law Review* (1976–77), 845–1154. The papers presented by prominent commentators during two conferences at the University of Alabama School of Law in 1985 and 1986 commemorating the centennial of the birth of Justice Black were published as, "Hugo L. Black: Alabamian and American, 1886–1937, Part I," 36 *Alabama Law Review* (Spring 1985), 789–926; and "Hugo L. Black: The Court Years, 1937–1971, Part II," 38 *Alabama Law Review* (Winter 1987), 215–494. These essays are edited with an introduction by Tony Freyer, in *Justice Hugo L. Black and Modern America* (Tuscaloosa, 1989).

Black's relation to Alabama Populism, Progressivism, and the Ku Klux Klan are important to any interpretation of his constitutional thought. The only academic overview of Black's years before joining the Court is Virginia Van der Ver Hamilton's fine work, *Hugo Black: The Alabama Years* (Baton Rouge, 1972). The value of Black's "Memoirs" should be considered in light of Hamilton's scholarship. At the same time, however, her own strong suggestions concerning the influence on Black of Populism, Progressivism, and the Klan must be considered in the context of the more critical perspective presented in Sheldon Hackney, "The Clay County Origins of Mr. Justice Black: The Populist as Insider," J. Mills Thornton, "Hugo Black and the Golden Age," Paul L. Murphy, "The Early Social and Political

Philosophy of Hugo Black: Liquor as a Test Case," and Bertram Waytt-Brown, "Ethical Background of Hugo Black's Career," 36 *Alabama Law Review* (Spring 1985), 835–844, 861–926. An excellent study of Alabama during the Populist and Progressive era is Sheldon Hackney, *Populism to Progressivism in Alabama* (Princeton, 1969). Carl V. Harris, *Political Power in Birmingham, 1871–1921* (Knoxville, 1977), is a superb study.

Taken together these works provide the basis for a comprehensive analysis of Black's involvement in the Ku Klux Klan, demonstrating that political expediency alone does not explain it. Crucial to this analysis is the significance of the prohibition crusade and the political culture it reflected, particularly as they shaped the relationship between Black's law practice and public career. Ball, "Justice Hugo L. Black: A Magnificent Product of the South," 36 *Alabama Law Review* (Spring 1985), also suggested this point.

Black's identification as one of the Senate's staunchest liberals was inseparable from his role in supporting Roosevelt's New Deal. Hamilton's *Alabama Years* examines in depth Black's ten-year Senate career, including the rise of New Deal liberalism. See also David A. Shannon, "Hugo La Fayette Black as United States Senator," 36 *Alabama Law Review* (Spring 1985), 881–898; and John P. Frank, "The New Court and the New Deal," Strickland, ed., *Black and the Supreme Court*. Studies of particular New Deal policies that include important references to Black are: Ellis W. Hawley, *The New Deal and the Problem of Monopoly: A Study in Economic Ambivalence* (Princeton, 1966); Stanley Vittoz, *New Deal Labor Policy and the American Industrial Economy* (Chapel Hill, 1987); Mark H. Leff, *The Limits of Symbolic Reform, The New Deal and Taxation, 1933–1939* (Cambridge, 1984); and James C. Cobb and Michael V. Namorato, eds., *The New Deal and the South* (Jackson, 1984). For the defeat of the Antilynch bill see Black's filibuster speech in 79 *Congressional Record* 6532 (April 29, 1935); and for Roosevelt's stance see Harvard Sitkoff, "The Impact of the New Deal on Black Southerners," in Cobb and Namorato, eds., *New Deal and the South*, 118.

The studies of Black's Court years are quite extensive. Thus only a selective list can be suggested as a guide to the larger literature. G. Edward White, *The American Judicial Tradition:*

Profiles of Leading American Judges (New York, 1976), places Black in the context of the Court's changing personalities and doctrines. Paul L. Murphy, *The Constitution in Crisis Times, 1918–1969* (New York, 1971), provides an overview of the period including Black's service up to the arrival of Chief Justice Warren E. Burger. Vincent Blasi, ed., *The Burger Court: The Counter Revolution That Wasn't* (New Haven, 1983), discusses Black's contribution to the initial years of the Burger Court. For the Warren Court years, nothing matches in detail and depth Bernard Schwartz, *Super Chief: Earl Warren and his Supreme Court—A Judicial Biography* (New York, 1983). The generally fine sketches of the Justices in Leon Friedman and Fred L. Israel, eds., *The Justices of the United States Supreme Court, 1789–1978* (5 vols., New York, 1969–78), supplement these other references, particularly for the period of Chief Justice Fred Vinson's tenure.

The best examinations of the struggle over Black's appointment to the Court, including the uproar accompanying the revelation of his former Klan membership, are Dunne, *Black and the Judicial Revolution,* and William E. Leuchtenburg, "A Klansman Joins the Court: The Appointment of Hugo L. Black," 41 *University of Chicago Law Review* (1973).

The references to Black in David J. Danelski and Joseph S. Tulchin, eds., *The Autobiographical Notes of Charles Evans Hughes* (Cambridge, 1973), are illuminating for Black's initial three years. Alpheus Thomas Mason, *Harlan Fiske Stone: Pillar of the Law* (New York, 1956), describes well the inner story of the Court during Black's first decade, though Stone's view of him was often critical. J. Woodford Howard, Jr., *Mr. Justice Murphy: A Political Biography* (Princeton, 1968), offers perhaps the leading example of a justice whose libertarianism exceeded Black's during the middle and late 1940s. These two works, moreover, provide an insider's account of the Court's Japanese-American internment and wartime enemies decisions, though the treatment of the former needs to be supplemented by Peter H. Irons, *Justice at War: The Inside Story of the Japanese American Internment* (New York, 1983). See also Tony Freyer, *Harmony & Dissonance:*

The Swift and Erie Cases in American Federalism (New York, 1981), for Black's contribution to Brandeis' paradoxical use of judicial activism to achieve self-restraint in the *Erie* decision.

For the Cold War struggles and the pioneering civil rights decisions of the postwar years there are several good specialized works. Walter F. Murphy, *Congress and the Court: A Case Study in the American Political Process* (Chicago, 1962), describes the influence of McCarthyism on the efforts to restrict the Court's jurisdiction. Maeva Marcus, *Truman and the Steel Seizure Case: The Limits of Presidential Power* (New York, 1977), is the best study of the *Youngstown* case, including Black's role. Dennis J. Hutchinson, "Unanimity and Desegregation: Decisionmaking in the Supreme Court, 1948–1958," 68 *The Georgetown Law Journal* (October 1979), 1–96, is the most detailed inside account of the Court's movement toward, decision in, and initial consequence of the revolutionary *Brown* v. *Board of Education* (1954). A broader work representing the perspective of the NAACP is the masterpiece by Richard Kluger, *Simple Justice: The History of Brown v. Board of Education and Black America's Struggle for Equality* (New York, 1977). Tony Freyer, *The Little Rock Crisis* (Westport, Conn., 1984), discusses the first major confrontation arising from the implementation of *Brown* II. See also Michael S. Mayer, "With Much Deliberation and Some Speed: Eisenhower and the *Brown* Decision," 52 *The Journal of Southern History* (February 1986), 43–76.

A fine study of the constitutional struggle for racial justice, including especially the role of the federal government from the late fifties to the late sixties, is Michal R. Belknap, *Federal Law and Social Order: Racial Violence and Constitutional Conflict in the Post-Brown South* (Athens, 1987). See also Juan Williams, *Eyes on the Prize: America's Civil Rights Years, 1954–1965* (New York, 1987), for a view by blacks themselves concerning the civil rights movement. A case study of the most important school desegregation decision during Black's brief tenure on the Burger Court is Bernard Schwartz, *Swann's Way: The School Busing Case and the Supreme Court* (New York, 1986). Two splendid books that probe the interaction of race, politics, and economics in the South during Black's life are: V. O. Key, Jr., *Southern Politics in State and Nation* (Knoxville, 1984); and Gavin Wright, *Old South, New South: Revolutions in the Southern Economy Since the Civil War* (New York, 1986).

Undoubtedly, the best introductions to Black's constitutional thought are the James Madison Lecture entitled "The Bill of Rights," appearing in *New York University Law Review* (April 1960), and the three Carpentier Lectures delivered at Columbia University (Spring 1968), published as *A Constitutional Faith* (New York, 1968). Frankfurter and Black were the object of many comparative studies exploring the relative merits of judicial activism and self-restraint. A more recent book that refers to and places earlier works in perspective is Mark Silverstein, *Constitutional Faiths, Felix Frankfurter, Hugo Black, and the Process of Judicial Decision Making* (Ithaca, 1984). For an introduction to the extensive literature on Black and free expression see John P. Frank, "Hugo L. Black: Free Speech and the Declaration of Independence," *University of Illinois Law Forum* (1977). An examination of the incorporation of the Bill of Rights into the Fourteenth Amendment can be found in Richard C. Cortner, *The Supreme Court and the Second Bill of Rights* (New York, 1981). For further discussions of these and Black's other constitutional doctrines see Strickland, ed., *Black and the Supreme Court*, and the two symposia published by *Alabama Law Review* and *Southwestern University Law Review* cited above.

Vital to my interpretation of Black's thought is the significance of his books. Daniel J. Meador, *Mr. Justice Black and His Books* (Charlottesville, 1974), is indispensable to any attempt to determine the influence of reading upon Black's ideas. The books themselves are located at the University of Alabama School of Law in a reproduction of Black's Alexandria home library. The study of the marginal notations in Black's books, combined with the citation of the same books in his opinions and published writings, led me to focus on the importance of unchanging human nature as central to Black's core values. This same material facilitated my use of Bertram Wyatt-Brown's insight concerning the importance of respectability; see "Ethical Background of Hugo Black's Career," 36 *Alabama Law Review* (Spring 1985).

For a criticism of Black and his ideas, see especially Sylvia Snowiss, "The Legacy of Justice Black," Philip B. Kurland, ed., *The Supreme Court Review* (Chicago 1973), 187–252, which has influenced me considerably; and John T. Noonan, Jr., Review of Dunne's *Black and the Judicial Revolution* in 9 *Southwestern Law Review* (1976–77), 1127–1137; Glendon Schubert, *The Constitutional Polity* (Boston, 1970); Leonard W. Levy, *Emergence of a Free Press* (New York, 1985), vii–xix; and Harry T. Edwards, "Justice Black and Labor Law," 38 *Alabama Law Review* (Spring 1987).

An up-to-date bibliography of publications by and about Justice Black, as well as a thorough listing of his opinions including brief summations of many of the most important ones, and a useful chronology of his life, is: Cherry Lynn Thomas and Jean McCulley Holcumb, "Hugo Lafayette Black: A Bibliography of the Court Years, 1937–1971," 38 *Alabama Law Review* (Winter 1987), 381–499. Black's opinions are to be found in volumes of the *United States Reports,* 302 U.S. (1937) to 403 U.S. (1971).

Index

F